Hospitality

An Ecclesiological Practice of Ministry

Freddy James Clark

Hamilton Books
A member of
THE ROWMAN & LITTLEFIELD PUBLISHING GROUP
Lanham · Boulder · New York · Toronto · Plymouth, UK

Copyright © 2007 by
Hamilton Books
4501 Forbes Boulevard
Suite 200
Lanham, Maryland 20706
Hamilton Books Acquisitions Department (301) 459-3366

Estover Road
Plymouth PL6 7PY
United Kingdom

Library of Congress Control Number: 2004115333
ISBN-13: 978-0-7618-2982-9 (paperback : alk. paper)
ISBN-10: 0-7618-2982-2 (paperback : alk. paper)

Contents

Foreword

"Hospitality" may be one of the greatest terms to be overlooked as a word and yet one of the most friendly usables in life.

Around the term "hospitality" we have the hospital, the hospice, the host, the hostel and the hostess. All of these refer or relate in some manner to *service* and accommodations, and kind treatment for others rather than self.

In this Christian view, as defined and described by Dr. Clark, we find that the basis of such human behavior stems from the heart of the people of God.

It is no wonder then that the Institutionalized Church will have Usher Groups and Ministries to serve this present age. A basic need is met when this ministry is performed. Pastor Clark has rendered us a Bible-based stance from which to justify and build a service which our Lord God promoted when He said that "the greatest among us must be a servant."

When you read this book you will be encouraged to double your efforts to "serve this present age."

Dr. L. K. Curry
Pastor Emeritus
Emmanuel Baptist Church
Chicago, Illinois

Foreword

My son in ministry, Dr. Freddy James Clark, "in whom I am well pleased," is a proven and distinguished prophet, pastor and pulpiteer. Now he gives us his unique ability as a writer by taking on the task of challenging the Christian community, at Shalom and elsewhere, to identify with true evangelization and its major component: *hospitality*.

This shepherd at Shalom Church looms upon the horizon as an elite manager of human resources properly discerning people, places and time. Servant Clark records the heart of true evangelization for the Christian Community—hospitality; only when a seed is sown in warm "*hospitable*-soil" does it germinate.

The writer challenges readers and church community to reach within ourselves and be "*hospitable*." To do as the Nazarene invited the John the Baptist committee, "Come and see." (Jn 1:39) Like Moses tried to entice his father-in-law, Jethro, "To come with us and it will do thee good."

The author is saying to us, the Christian community, that *hospitality* is to evangelization what the Rosetta Stone proved to be to the Egyptian civilization.

With this degree of understanding *hospitality*, the 21st century Christian community might have some possible identity with the 1st Century Church, by prodding us in this 21st Century to recapture the "clarion" distinctive of "how they loved one another." One must love the stranger, the guest and the uninvited in order to live out the mandate of He who came to reconcile the so-called lost.

Inspired by this writing, maybe the Faith Community can learn from the marketplace around them . . . saying "May I help you?" "The light stays on for you." "Good Morning." "We are here to please you." "Your comfort is our joy."

Looking for church growth? Try digesting and implementing this genius of hospitality—*Hospitality—An Ecclesiological Practice of Ministry.*

I challenge you, Dr. Clark, to go the next step and develop a study guide to this great literary text. We will be ever indebted to you. I know in the African-American Baptist community, we thirst for this kind of leadership. We applaud your insight and accomplishment.

A-men.

Moses Javis
Continuing Pastor, Mt. Olive Baptist of Webster, Florida
Residing in Leesburg, Florida

Preface

The Doctor of Ministry project focuses on hospitality as an ecclesiological practice of ministry at the Shalom Church. The Shalom Church, which views hospitality as a gift, seeks not to control the gift but to share and celebrate the gift in practice. When the practice is intentional it will become embedded in one's lifestyle. Making this practice second nature is to consider hospitality as a biblical and moral obligation, where every encounter with the other will be viewed through the lens of hospitality.

Fortunately, humanity always moves from host/stranger to stranger/host. In Christian theology the giver and receiver are one of equal regard. Since there are no permanent positions in life, persons are always moving in and out of situations where they experience sometimes being the host, and other times the stranger. Hospitality becomes the means by which equal regard and moral obligation are exercised.

Proclamation is the tool that shapes the practice and develops covenant relationship with hospitality as an embedded practice.

Acknowledgments

I want to acknowledge God in Whose Spirit I live, move and have my being. Without God none of this would be possible.

To Dr. Peggy Way and Dr. Enoch Oglesby, whose inspiration and guidance gave me constant direction in bringing this task to completion. Thank you!

To Erline Waller, Cynthia Rochester, Valerie McNeal and Patricia Tomlin, whose gifts and support I have had to depend upon in times when challenges became unbearable. Thank you!

To the entire Shalom Church Family, particularly the ministerial staff and church schoolteachers whose prayers have been both heard and felt, to you I owe so much.

Lastly, to my wonderful wife, Cheryl and my children, Terrence, Anthony and Michelle—you mean the world to me. Your understanding and support have been the reasons I have excelled in every challenge. You are truly the wind beneath my wings.

I love you!

Introduction

What does hospitality look like at the Shalom Church? This is the central thrust of this work. It has been said that the Shalom Church has the gift of hospitality. However, more than just isolated incidents of hospitality, I have been interested in hospitality becoming a deliberate theological ministerial practice. My pursuit of this ideal stems from realizing that gifts given are for the edifying of congregational life, and to a larger degree, for life in the context of the community in which the church finds itself. Therefore, when I speak in terms of Shalom Church having the gift of hospitality, I will be talking about not only having the gift recognized and celebrated but also grounded in the gospel of Jesus Christ, the ecclesiological practice of the congregation.

Moreover, if the Shalom Church has the gift of hospitality, and working as a core group under this premise, how might it move from the core to the fringes of operating in a deliberate ministerial practice? How might it become more hospitable to the neighborhood? What are the necessary steps to take in developing a methodology by which other church leaders can see and begin to make hospitality a part of the shared practical experience in ministry?

Being a pastor, and in the context of worship, believing that preaching is central, what place does the gospel (proclamation) have in shaping individuals to honor the other, even when their "otherness" is radically at odds with their beliefs? These are the issues I hope to make a connection with in providing a context for hospitality that is deliberate and ongoing in the practice of ministry at the Shalom Church.

Chapter I

Forming A
New Historical Narrative

The organizing of this Christian fellowship can be viewed as the formation of a new historical community. How I have come to understand the Shalom Church experience, as a local congregation, is due [in part] to our journey. Spending eighteen months looking for a permanent place to worship; from the Holiday Inn to Ascension Catholic Church gymnasium, to our present location in Berkeley, Missouri, worship happened! For six months, individuals faithfully attended worship services every Sunday in the basement of the Holiday Inn. However, this was a strange yet challenging phenomenon for these faithful.

First, there was the obvious; wanting to worship but not being around the familiar signs and symbols of the church that make worship comfortable, the Lord's Supper table, the banners, the cross; all that were always so visible. We were in a strange land playing by the rules of the landlord, Holiday Inn. We pushed our way with all of our theological sound bytes such as "It's not in the land, it's in the man" trying to convince ourselves that place did not matter, only the people in the place. But somehow we knew deep down in our souls that place did matter, and the place that we were in was not our place but a temporary stop on our way to a place that God had for us.

Every Saturday evening we would meet to get our rented space ready for worship-provided a social event had not been booked. If there was a social activity scheduled for Saturday night, some of us would agree to be in place early Sunday before worship to ensure that everything was in place. The podium, along with chairs for the choir area and chairs for the worshippers were put in place. This remained consistent for six weeks. As the pastor of this new faith community, I must admit that I never knew what to expect from our group or the proprietors of the establishment. I had not been able to persuade the Holiday Inn to give us a binding contract that would ensure three-month increments of time. They were only willing to do a week-to-week agreement. So there were times when I would arrive not knowing whether or not we would be able to rent space. I was also burdened by the thought of the people tiring.

It was (I thought) a lot to ask of them to exist as nomads for an undetermined amount of time. I did not know how long this pace could be maintained with many of them already leading full lives. But much to my surprise, they remained committed to being a new faith community. We had been a fellowship for about four weeks. Now, in the Baptist tradition, which all of us were a part of, our polity required that you unite with the church in order to be considered a member of the church.

Up to this point, the Shalom Church had no new members. No one had united because I had not given an invitation to membership. Here's why: We had just left a very emotionally charged atmosphere. Persons who had made the decision to leave (follow) were very invested in the history of this place in the form of family, friends, and memories. Strained by the *confusion* and the *disconnection,* I wanted to make sure that after creating some distance, they had an opportunity to think clearly, to reflect upon the decision and return if they so desired—feeling no obligation to anyone but God. These four weeks, I had hoped would be substantial time to make a decision. I believed it would grant enough time for the "dust to settle." However, on the fifth week, when the invitation for membership was given, there were 253 people who stood and vowed their commitments to this community and renewed their convictions to Christ. Many of these people (I thought) would not make the journey. This could not have been more timely or divinely orchestrated because shortly thereafter, our weekly arrangement with the Holiday Inn was terminated.

While at the Holiday Inn, although our stay was brief, there was an emerging articulated understanding of worship and public life. The Holiday Inn had an ongoing narrative that included housing the stranger overnight with the stranger having the right to roam the building if he/she so chose; that roaming included our worship as well. We entered the Holiday Inn with the thought of occupying space that was "for us." We had not really thought about the worship experience being "for all" but just "for us." Yet, while being the strangers in a strange place, we began to entertain strangers in the worship experience. Those who were in the hotel as guests, as we were, heard the music, the singing, the praying, and the preaching, and they decided to enter the worship. Perhaps we were seeking community as an escape from constraints we had experienced and were comfortable being self-contained.

However, concerns grew because the unknown "others" invaded our worship space. We imagine the church as family, a family where intimacy and trust would be known without reservation, where we could exist without conflict, and if conflict arose, it could be handled with little or no difficulty because everybody is known. It was just us! However, God was doing something else with us and I venture to say, God was doing something in us. What we thought was private and personal had become public and communal. The worship experience was no longer something that was simply for a people who called themselves "Shalom."

But in and through worship, shalom was being created for the larger community that existed in the Holiday Inn Hotel and beyond. Although our stay at the hotel was brief, our memory of having made friends of strangers and having lost our privacy, has been lasting. There is now a new understanding of how dangerous self-containment can be for communities that will serve to witness to the Lordship of Jesus Christ in the world.

This would be an important lesson to learn, because upon leaving the hotel, our journey took us to Ascension Catholic Church gymnasium. If one can worship in a hotel, we thought, one can worship anywhere—even at the gym. One thing we quickly discovered in the gym was a lack of luxury. There were no carpeted floors, no cushioned chairs (as in the hotel) and during the winter months of our stay, we had very little heat. However, the intensity of worship was warming and transforming for all. It took several weeks to make the adjustment to our "new home."

In the adjustment, we experienced the many surprising ways God will show up while in the wilderness. As we were growing, both numerically and spiritually, and having our identity shaped by our landless condition, the larger Christian community [from which we were now estranged] was busy casting shadows of hostility, shame and false propaganda. As this persisted, there was a feeling of abandonment by God, as well as many others to whom we had given so much of ourselves. Yet, even with this before us, we knew that we could not exist in isolation nor did we want to.

We needed the shared experiences of other fellowships, because life is lived, historically, in the context of others. However, there were few, if any, who wanted to risk being our friend. We later discovered that other Christians found our name problematic in the sense that many thought somehow we were duly aligned with the Nation of Islam, or Black Muslims, headed by the Minister Louis Farrakhan. We were not part of the Islamic tradition by any means. I do not say this as a form of condescension, only clarity! There were questions that began to surface in the fellowship about our name "Shalom." We soon realized that "Shalom" was not a typical name for a black church, and how easy it was for our detractors to attempt to connect us with a movement that was not Christ-centered simply by distorting the name. However, this gave us a marvelous opportunity to enlighten and encourage the congregation on the actual meaning of "Shalom." This was a new name for a new people.

I was inspired by the shalom concept and adopted it as the name of our fellowship while preaching a collection of sermons from John's gospel concerning Jesus' farewell address from the table. Indeed, one may find the name Shalom to be unique as it is not in the Bible but the entire Bible can be used as a shalom text. Shalom means *peace*, not only in the sense of freedom from disturbing conflict, but in totality: health, wholeness, harmony, success and the complete richness of living in a wholesome fellowship with others. From the misunderstanding and conflict that was being created from without, a purpose statement was developed from within.

We developed a purpose statement to reflect our desire to live toward this end.

It reads:

The purpose of Shalom Church (City of Peace) shall be the maintenance of Christian work and worship for the complete spiritual, mental and physical growth, nurture and improvement of the local manifestation of the Universal Church through which Jesus Christ continues to minister to the world by His Holy Spirit. The fellowship of Shalom Church (City of Peace) shall promote health, wholesomeness, and harmony in

> *its manifestation of the faith and fellowship to which God has called God's people. We shall seek to fulfill this calling through the conversion of the lost; corporate worship services; a program of Christian nurture by which our fellowship may be built up in faith and love; opportunity for service by the application of the gifts with which God has blessed our fellowship; proclamation and teaching of the Gospel of Jesus Christ by word and deed; and, through ministering to human need with prayer and provision, in the name of Jesus Christ, a wholesome environment in which we fellowship and serve.*

Although the purpose statement may be lengthy for some, it provides a means to teach precisely what this fellowship is about and, at the same time, calm some fears about our not being Christ-centered.

In the teaching, I cited several things about our name "Shalom" that I thought were important. Furthermore, I wanted to ease the tension for those trying to understand this name. This is the approach I used in attempting to teach how our fellowship was being shaped:

> First, the vision of Shalom Church (City of Peace) is to embrace Ephesians 2:14: "For He Himself is our peace, Who made both groups into one and broke down the barrier of the dividing wall." Secondly, we live out our personal commitment in the context of the "other." This concern for the "other" is not what I witnessed in the church from which we were removed. Shalom Church would be about embracing the differences of the other and rejoicing in diversity so unity could happen!

The vision is two-pronged—on one hand, experiencing joy, well-being, harmony and prosperity; on the other, becoming visibly annoyed at persons who attempt to build walls that divide.

The atmosphere was so dangerous and destructive when we were leaving the other church, I thought our time in the gym was a good time for purging our consciousness of anything that did not invite community. Therefore, the concept of simple mutual respect became an important teaching piece in the understanding of shalom. Therein lies the third principle that was taught.

We should exhaust every means necessary to get along with brothers and sisters; by doing so, we honor God. Knowing that when others are valued, it brings value to oneself and to the human family.

It was also important to teach that the vision moves toward reality when persons resist all forms of coercion and manipulation, and seek to please God. These were some of the basic tenets of teaching about the vision of Shalom that happened in the gym. In explaining the name "Shalom," I felt it was important to make a biblical connection with the name. As previously stated, the word "shalom" is not in the Bible, but the entire Bible can be used as a shalom text. For instance, in the Old Testament, the Hebrew word shalom had a community thrust. The well-being of the community was first and foremost, seen to be over, against, and at the expense of the well-being of the other tribes. Shalom in the Bible (as a concept) was all about the creation of a community. Shalom was also a greeting or blessing as seen in Numbers 6:24–26:

> *The Lord bless you and keep you;*
> *The Lord Make His face to shine*
> *upon you, and be gracious to you;*
> *The Lord lift up His Countenance*
> *upon you and give you peace.*

When this was understood in the life of our church many persons greet each other using the word "shalom." Along with shalom being a greeting and blessing, it has a strong bias

toward the poor and oppressed. Therefore, anyone who was
denied this thrust became the subject of concern. Jeremiah
29:7 says,

> But seek the welfare of the city where
> I have sent you into exile, and pray to
> The Lord on its behalf: for in its welfare,
> You will have welfare.

In seeking and praying for shalom where Israel was in exile,
they themselves, will have shalom. I am of the opinion that
wilderness and *exile* give one the sensitivity necessary to em-
body shalom. Shalom can mean many things but to our fellowship, it is not accidental. The way we define it makes sense
in the context of our struggle. Also, it is worth mentioning that
the idea of justice, which is very important, is not divorced
from the notion of shalom, but a necessary expression of how
shalom is to be practiced. Martin Luther King, Jr. and other
civil rights champions, when talking about justice, often referred to the prophet Amos who said,

> *Let Justice roll down like water and righteousness like a mighty*
> *stream.*
>
> Amos 5:24

The point is clearly made that the absence of justice is an absence of shalom. The Old Testament retains and frames the
meaning of shalom around the concept of wholeness, well-
being, concern for the poor and oppressed and justice for
humanity.

In the New Testament gospels, there are all kinds of shalom
situations created by Jesus. In the gospel of Mark, there is first
the storm narrative. This is followed by the remarkable exchange between Jesus and the man called Legion in Mark
5:1–15. In staying with chapter five of Mark there is the issue

of both Jarius and a woman who had a hemorrhage. I do not seek to do an exegesis on any of the passages mentioned, but simply to share that in all of these places a sense of order (shalom) was restored by honoring the basic need for the person at that time.

Theologically, shalom is both gift and goal. The gift of shalom is shared in the context of the community that operated on trust and common bonding that ties persons together. The whole community must participate; each person is to make a contribution to the whole that there be nothing lacking. The model that was taught while in the Ascension Catholic Church Gymnasium, is Paul's model in I Corinthians 12, where he stresses the importance of every spiritual gift working for the common good of the whole.

Now concerning spiritual gifts; brethren I do not want you to be uninformed. You know that when you were heathen, you were led astray to the dumb idols however you may have been moved. Therefore, I want you to understand that no one speaking by the spirit of God ever says, "Jesus be cursed!" And that no one can say "Jesus is Lord," except by the Holy Spirit. Now there are varieties of gifts, but the same Spirit. And there are varieties of service but the same Lord. And there are varieties of working, but it is the same God who inspires them all in everyone. To each one is given the manifestation of the spirit for the common good. To one is given through the spirit the utterance of wisdom, and to another the utterance of knowledge according to the same spirit. To another, faith by the same Spirit, and to another, gifts of healing by the one Spirit. To another the working of miracles, and to another prophecy and to another the ability to distinguish between spirits, to another various kinds of tongues, and to another the interpretation of tongues. All these are inspired by one and the same spirit, who apportions to each one individually as he wills. For just as the body is one and yet has many members, and all the members of

the body, though many, are one body, so also is with Christ. For by one Spirit we were all baptized into one body. Jews or Greeks, slaves or free- and all were made to drink of one Spirit.
I Corinthians 12 RSV

These are all parts working in concert with each other fostering what shalom should look like. The parts are not interchangeable but complementary.

Time seemed to pass swiftly in the gymnasium. The parish priest was often kind enough to make sure that we had enough space to live out our calling in this in-between place. However, it soon became clear that even he could not grant us the space that was needed because some way, somehow, this church operating with this strange name, formulating this new narrative, was attracting people from everywhere. When asked, "What was the attraction?" The response was "freedom of worship, sense of community and the attitude of hospitality."

Here is this new community that is landless or in-between places, being nurtured by God and in return, nurturing persons who stopped by without intentions of staying, but stayed because their needs were met in the encounter, their need for an authentic worship, their need for a community that was accepting, and their need for hospitality. It was no longer just us as it had been months prior to this in the hotel. It was full of others with different narratives and different levels of understanding with one thing in common, as Anthony Jones says, "being committed to something God has God's hands on."[1] They were committed to being a part of a church that offers alternatives for experiencing God in new ways.

Now, there were not, at Shalom Church, any new ways of experiencing God. We simply clarified what was already in place traditionally through preaching, teaching and praying and through these vehicles an awareness of what many already knew intellectually was now being experienced emotionally and later viscerally. In all, the gymnasium served as a tremendous place of preparation for what God was revealing to Shalom Church in a broader context, an ongoing sensitivity that is needed to do ministry. We were really becoming a people of covenant. There was a love for God and a visible love for one another. We not only revisited the Standard Baptist Church Covenant but in keeping with all things new, we developed another covenant that we hope will (in years to come) speak and remind others of what it means to be a community that practiced the principles of shalom. This is what the covenant says:

It being made manifest by God's word that God is pleased to walk in the way of covenant with God's people, God promising to be our God and we promising to be God's people: We, therefore, desiring to worship and serve God, and believing it to be our duty to walk together as one body in Christ, do freely and solemnly covenant with God and with one another, and do bind ourselves in the presence of God, to acknowledge God to be our God and we to be God's people; to cleave unto the Lord Jesus, the Great Head of the Church, as our only King and Savior; and to walk together in Christian harmony, the spirit of God assisting us, in all God's ways and ordinances as they have been made known or shall be made known unto us from the Holy scripture; praying that the God of peace, Who brought from the dead, our Lord Jesus, may prepare and strengthen us for every good work, working in us that which is well pleasing in God's sight, through Jesus Christ our Lord, to Whom be glory and power forever and ever. Amen.

As we transitioned from the gymnasium to the Berkeley location, there was time to pause and reflect over the previous eighteen months of our journey in the wilderness, and how that journey connected to this work on the practice of hospitality. One of the surprising things that the core group of Shalom Church came to realize was that while in the wilderness, accommodations were always met and sometimes through the

unexpected. Many times God used the stranger to go above
and beyond his duty to be hospitable. It was in the hotel that
the strangers taught us that worship was a public act that
needed to be shared with a public that was fragmented and in-
dividualized. It was in the gymnasium that the parish priest
who played the host made sure that space was provided and the
freedom was given for us to live out the calling as a people of
faith whose theological context was different from their own.

It is possible, I believe upon reflection, that from our name
Shalom Church (City of Peace) and our challenges as a wilderness-wandering people, an awareness of hospitality began to
emerge as a ministerial practice. While in Berkeley, Missouri
with carpeted floors, cushioned pews and a steeple, we refused
to forget how God used human hands to help us along the way.

In the larger context we also remembered another people
whose story of wilderness dwelling provided an outlet to help
us understand our own narrative. Israel's experience of landlessness and scarcity, which doesn't end, became the strongest
biblical motif shaping our identity. Walter Brueggemann[2], in
his book, *The Land*, addresses the issue of Israel's situation. He
asserts the following: "Exodus 16 is a story about landlessness
and about surprise manna given and received so that wilderness is discerned as a place of surprising expectation and unexpected resources." He further states, "In the wilderness, Yahweh provides when there seems to be no available provision.
Life is rooted in impossibility. Landlessness is a condition in
which the land promised sustains His people . . . Yahweh has
acted in landlessness to provide for His people, just enough for
life."

Landlessness is what the Israelites experienced on their way
to the Promised Land, but landlessness provided a new historical narrative for Israel, because landlessness became the surprise in the journey.

They were leaving Egypt on their way to the Promised Land, but wilderness happened. Wilderness is that in-between place Yahweh used to formulate a new historical narrative with people who had no place. Wilderness became the shaping tool Yahweh used in helping Israel understand how it, not by any other power or might but by and through Yahweh, would exist. To be sure, Israel had its moment of feeling abandoned. It is strongly depicted in Exodus 16:

> *The whole congregation of the Sons of Israel grumbled against Moses and Aaron in the wilderness. The sons of Israel said to them, "Would that we had died by the Lord's hand in the Land of Egypt, when we sat by the pots of meat, when we ate bread to the full; for you have brought us out into this wilderness to kill this whole assembly with hunger."*

Their protest is not only against Moses, Aaron and hunger, but also against their displacement as well as against wilderness. Wilderness for them, as they perceived it, is the way to death. They were right in their assessment because wilderness is always a reshaping of life's agenda that produces death for the sake of the new alternatives for life.

The surprise of provision in the wilderness is interesting and exciting. For in the wilderness provisions were made, needs were met, the unexpected happened. Yahweh miraculously provided. Yahweh hosted a banquet in the wilderness, demonstrating that Yahweh has the power to sustain.

> *The Lord said to Moses, "Behold, I will rain bread from heaven for you; and the people shall go out and gather a day's portion every day that I may prove them whether they will walk in my law, or not."*

Exodus 16:4 (NAS)

Israel is not abandoned in the wilderness. Yahweh has not left them to fend for themselves. He is their shepherd, they shall not want.

Without overly romanticizing the shalom narrative with that of Israel's wilderness-wandering narrative, I will reflect on several dynamics. As a result of being a wilderness people who were forming a new community narrative, a sensitivity to the stranger emerged as a ministerial practice. That sensitivity is explicitly in the form of hospitality at the Shalom Church. Because we were shown hospitality, there is, I think, an obligation to now demonstrate hospitality.

Finally, this could not have happened if we, like Israel, had not become a landless people. Life as we once had it, shaped by conventions, moderators and precedents, was no more. We, like Israel, came to know that certain histories end. When history ends, people become hopelessly caught in between. However, the good news is that the God of history gives new beginnings. God allows us to see that we stop only to start over again. God has the power to energize a new community narrative. The one who tears down can build up and the one who plucks can plant; this is one of the extraordinary things about God, as He remains active in human history, whether the history of Israel, Shalom Church or any fellowship that finds itself estranged by the formalities of complacency.

In the next chapter I want to look at hospitality as a moral and biblical obligation to be practiced by the Shalom Church in response to God's grace demonstrated while we were in the wilderness formation.

Chapter II

Hospitality is a Moral and Biblical Obligation

In the previous chapter where hospitality was defined and celebrated as a form of God's grace demonstrated to the Shalom Church community while in the wilderness of formation, Shalom emerged from their experience with determination to share with others the gift they had received themselves, that of hospitality. Here I will argue that hospitality to the stranger is a moral and biblical obligation. Hospitality when shared is more than simply entertaining guests with kindness, which is a secular definition of the word. However, when interpreted theologically it becomes a paradigm for understanding the moral richness and biblical obligations, which are associated with hospitality. In this chapter, I will consider hospitality as a deliberate practice, a moral perspective, and a spiritual discipline. All of these are important in understanding the practice of ministry at Shalom Church.

The moral life is exceedingly rich and complex. Being able to answer the call to moral obligation depends largely on how much one is willing to remember of the peculiarities of his/ her journey personally and collectively. Being a stranger in an alien place, confused, needing some kind of reliable assurance, is not a new phenomena; how the stranger is treated is

of concern because all of us are always moving in circles that
are sometimes strange to us. It is interesting that one can understand a situation ethically and yet make the wrong moral
choice. However, the church has stood historically as a moral
compass to guide persons along the way. For moral development to happen, and this is true of any development, one has
to be rooted and sensitized to these things. If there is no foundational understanding of one's roots, there will be aimless
wanderings, just as a long trip without a destination. Knowing
who we are requires knowing the tradition by which we live,
and the tradition from which we came. Moral understanding
requires being part of a history and being aware of it as a part
of our core. For the Shalom Church to understand hospitality
as a paradigm for moral obligation it must make a connection
with the community of her ethnicity.

That ethnicity is the black community in which the church
is situated. Traditionally, the black church has been the symbol
of community, the house of hope, the place of character building and a city of refuge. It is from this tradition that we have
been nurtured and it is with this community that we share a
collective memory.

Moreover, the black church historically has been a source
of moral influence. The black church is more than just a
weekly pause in the busy quotidian events of the black
agenda. It is more than a spiritual filling station where some
look to hear theological sound bytes that send chills down their
spines. The black church is that institution that empowers
black people by informing them of their "isness" through the
medium of the word of God. The black church also affirms that
God has not been eclipsed by the systematic evil of this
world; that God is still in charge and yet remains on the side of
the oppressed. Because of this truth, there is no reason for the
church to shrink from its responsibility of moral obligation as
an agent of action, producing spiritual and social transforma-

tion. In the next pages, I will both illustrate and ground that understanding.

THE BLACK CHURCH AS AN AGENT OF ACTION

There is a certain comfort and complacency that accompanies arrival. Arrival has a way of taking away the cutting edge of a vibrant vision. However, the ideal of hospitality as an obligation and moral responsibility can help keep the perspective in focus. The church should not be a self-serving institution, but instead should mirror the life of Jesus Christ as well as honoring the "otherness" of God's creation. When the church understands that it exists for Christ and for the sake of Christ's mission in the world, it will become an agent of action.

However, to take action without having information about one's own identity would be a tragic mistake. To prepare for action it takes more than sharing common geography, or a common story from shared experiences. It is the constant rehearsal and retelling of those events, connecting them with the biblical narrative, which shapes the community for action. Larry Rassmussen expresses the view of the church as an agent of action in the following: "the formation of moral identity, utilizing moral tradition in the process, is a crucial role of the faith community as is moral deliberation, also using these traditions. Yet, conscience and character formation and deliberation of issue aren't ends in themselves. They exist to serve concrete action."[3] Now, to understand this practicality is to suggest that the test of any moral truth is in the social forms it embraces, and the difference it makes after the embracing. When taking this into consideration, hospitality as a moral obligation has a pro-formative role. It's an action word much like that of faith, reconciliation, liberation, forgiveness and social involvement. It's pro-formative. One cannot practice hospitality without spiritual nurturing.

However, in making this assertion as it relates to being pro-formative, Rasmussen also states "that moral action assumes that agents are aware of what they are doing, have some knowledge they feel is appropriate to the action, have some purpose in mind for the action, and have some possibility for acting."[4] In respect to the church functioning morally, Rasmussen has two starting points. The first he calls "Home Turf," that is the faith community's starting point for moral discourse. It is both the subject and the object of the social ethic it claims and proclaims. For instance, if in the Eucharist it is proclaimed that all are welcomed and in the world, we all share one common loaf and drink from one common cup and belong together as one in the family of God, and then we turn around and disallow someone the privilege of sharing in the meal because of some human discrepancy, something is wrong. Also, when forms of discrimination surface against divorcees or someone whose sexual orientation is different from our own, something is wrong. For moral development to happen, one has to be rooted and sensitive to the many ways in which humanity exists regardless of one's own personal bias, for the sake of community.

Secondly, he states in *"The Wider Public,"* that the second zone of moral obligation and action is the world beyond the walls of the institutional church. The actor is still the faith community with its focus on the external of the public arena. This is not the action of a few, but this is the church's action as a corporate agent, making a corporate witness in the world. He uses the rationale of Karl Barth to make his point:

"The decisive contribution which the Christian community can make to up-building, work and maintenance of the civil order consists in the witness which it has to give to it and all human societies in the form of its own up-building and con-stitution. It cannot give, in the world, a direct portrayal of Jesus Christ, who is also the world's Lord and Savior, or the peace and freedom and joy of the Kingdom of God. For it is of itself only a human society, moving like all others to God's manifestation. But the form in which it exists among them can and must be to the world around it, a reminder of the law of the Kingdom of God, which is already set up on earth in Jesus Christ, and a promise of its future manifestations. De facto, whether they realize it or not, can, and should show them there is already on earth an order which is based on the great alternative of the human situation and directed toward its manifestation."[5]

As I follow the thinking of Birch and Rasmussen, I also know that one cannot practice morality as a disciple of Jesus Christ without seeing the liberating work of the ministry. Moreover, one cannot practice hospitality without having been liberated to be a participant in the liberating work of Jesus Christ. Hospitality, as a practice of ministry at the Shalom Church, must start with the liberating word and work of Jesus Christ. As Jesus goes, so goes the church. James Cone, in *A Black Theology of Liberation* suggests: "Participation in the historical liberation spearheaded by God is the defining characteristic of the church."[6] There are three defining charac-teristics Cone offers to support this claim.

First he says, "The church that is about the liberation must claim the reality of liberation." That liberation and the reality of its results, happens when the church preaches the liberating message of Jesus Christ. To have this message and not share this message would serve as a delay to what Christ hopes to do in using human instrumentality for the work of liberation. Jesus says in essence, now that you have the pouring out of the Holy Spirit,

*Go therefore and make disciples of all nations, baptizing them
in the name of the Father, Son, and Holy Spirit, teaching them
to observe all that I have commanded you; and lo, I am with
you always, to the close of the age.*

                                                      Matthew 28:19–20 RSV

Secondly, Cone claims, "The church not only proclaims the
good news of freedom, it actively shares in the liberating struggle."[7] He is suggesting that there is an ongoing battle in the
world (which does not want to give up its oppressive forces) to
inform them that persons who have received the gospel of
Jesus Christ, now live under new management. To share in the
liberating "struggle" is to understand its eschatological nature.
It is to understand that God is still working. The emancipator
has come and has done His part, and those of us who have been
liberated, share in the work and struggle. However, there are
some strongholds that are heavily entrenched but are coming
to an end. Until then, the Apostle Paul writes in Ephesians
6:10–18 as an encouragement and a warning to be aware that
God is still working.

*Finally, be strong in the Lord and in the strength of His
might. Put on the whole armor of God, so that you will be
able to stand against the wiles of the devil. For our struggle
is not contending against flesh and blood but against the
rulers, against the principalities, against the powers, against
the world rulers of this present darkness, against the spiritual hosts of wickedness in heavenly places. Therefore, take
the whole armor of God, that you will be able to withstand
in the evil day, and having done all to stand. Stand therefore,
having girded your loins with truth and having put on the
breastplate of righteousness and having shod your feet with
the equipment of the gospel of peace: besides all these, taking the shield of faith with which you can quench all the
flaming darts of the evil one.*

And take the helmet of salvation, and the sword of the Spirit, which is the word of God. Pray at all times in the Spirit, with all prayer and supplication for all the saints.

Ephesians 6:10-18

The third piece that Cone uses to characterize a liberating church is this: the church as a fellowship is a visible manifestation that the gospel is a reality. If the church is not free, if it lives to the reality of the old order, then it is a distortion. To believe is to live according to the gospel of Jesus Christ.

As I do a comparative analysis for moral grounding for practice strategies in the Shalom Church, Rasmussen and Birch, along with Lane, agree that the first move for developing persons for the liberating work of hospitality is in-house, introspection.

Also, they agree that the next necessary move after the nurturing and introspection of the church is the wider public. Cone says proclamation, as divine liberation, is the effective means for social protest. However, although these words may differ in explaining moral development, the starting point for both is that of the faith community.

Cone suggests "that when the good news of God's liberating freedom is heard and embraced, it becomes the responsibility of the liberated to share in the struggle of liberation."[8] However, Rasmussen and Birch perhaps are not thinking in terms of individual liberation resulting in community participation. What they envision with the term "The Wider Public" is the church's action as a corporate agent making corporate witness to what ought to happen in the world beyond the walls of the church.

While this may be true, it is Cone's third characteristic that calls into question everything that has been agreed upon to this point. He says, "The church as a fellowship is a visible manifestation that the gospel is a reality. If the church is not free, if

it is a distorted representation of the eruption of God's kingdom, it lives according to the old order; then no one will believe its message."[9] To believe is to live accordingly.

In essence, Cone is suggesting that the first two priorities or
strategies do not matter if who we are presiding over does not
believe the gospel. He argues that to really believe in the
gospel will produce evidence. That evidence is liberation. So if
the church has not been fully liberated by the power of the
gospel of Jesus Christ when there is opportunity for a "Wider
Public," they will have *presence* with no *power.* "No power because the power of this world still lays claims on them, one
cannot serve two masters; for either he will hate the one and
love the other, or he will be devoted to one and despise the
other. You cannot serve God and wealth."[10] Matthew 6:24

The church is the community that participates in Jesus
Christ's liberating work in history. Therefore it can never en-
force law that causes human suffering. Further, the church,
when liberated, must be a revolutionary community, breaking
laws and creating new ones that are inclusive of all humanity.

Cone's point rings clear—we have the tools and the intel-
lectual ability to address ourselves effectively to what is new
and evocative while retaining the assurance of what is known,
settled and traditional; yet giving the appearance of change
while we continue clinging to our egos and institutions. But
liberation, like hospitality, takes on a pro-formative role when
released through persons who have experienced the gospel of
Jesus Christ. Liberation enables them to not only appreciate
the nurturing elements in-house, but to reach beyond the walls
of the church into the wider public.

I turn now to an understanding of the black church as
moral discourse, utilizing the work of E. Hammond Oglesby to
address what is important in this work. This will illustrate further that an effective outreach happens because persons take

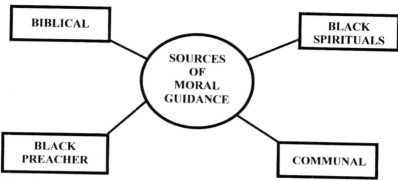

Figure 2.1

seriously effective in-reach. Now let us consider the components of the model illustrated in figure 2.1.

Enoch Oglesby asserts: "In the black Christian community, the scheme or orientational typology attempts to partially describe the dynamic patterns of interaction between the biblical and communal, the black spirituals and black preachers as sources and resources of ethical and moral guidance in the black community life."[11] After having looked closely at

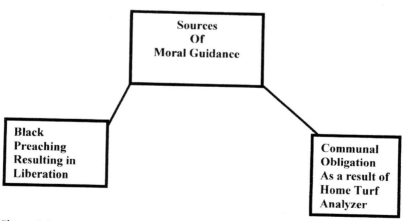

Figure 2.2

Oglesby's orientational typology model of "moral guidance," keeping in mind the contribution of Cone, Rasmussen and Barth, he has added perspectives and structures to a model that was incomplete and has given the model a sense of wholeness.

For instance, the model that was before us, up to this point, looked like figure 2.2.

The biblical and the black spiritual piece have been added, thus giving the model arms while having the ability to reach out and touch.

My concern is how the black church can be hospitable in both its inner and public life as illustrated in figure 2.3.

It is critical that persons not view preaching and Bible study as one. Preaching evokes inspiration to persons who perhaps have not opened the Bible, whereas Bible study or scripture rehearsal serves as a form of gathering information. One gives inspiration/preaching, the other gives information/Bible. Both deepen and ground the congregation's understanding of its obligations and practices.

Now, I will spend some time presenting a biblical basis for the practice of hospitality. The Bible is our primary source in the black church to receive information about God, Jesus, Holy Spirit, and the church. This would have no bearing on how Jesus is viewed. The preacher who may in preparation use the tools of form, redaction and historical criticism, would do well not to be impressive in preaching but simply tell the story.

Biblical **Bible Study and** **Scripture** **Interpretation**	**Black Spiritual** **Expression** **Of the** **Soul**

Figure 2.3

Oglesby says, "the Bible for blacks has always served as a central source, as well as a normative resource for Christian moral life. In the life of the black Christian community, the Bible is perceived not simply as *a* book, but *the* book, wherein the oppressed meet God in their suffering and toils and this Almighty God is perceived to give not only freedom but residual moral guidance to the children of dark skin."[12]

James Cone, in *God of the Oppressed*, says, "Blacks have intuitively drawn the all important distinction between infallibility and reliability. They have not contended for a fully explicit infallibility, feeling perhaps that there is mystery in the book as there is in Christ. What they have testified to is in the book's reliability: how it is the true and basic source for discovering the truth of Jesus Christ."[13] As Oglesby has said, not *a book*, but *the book*.

I list three passages which I think are important in the shaping of biblical discourse and for moral guidance as it relates to hospitality. It is important in the black church that the Jesus who is met in scripture is not reduced to somebody who can be comfortably controlled. Let's hear what the book says.

In the beginning was the Word, and the Word was God. He was in the beginning with God. All things were made through
Him and without Him was not anything made that was made. In Him was life, and the life was the light of men. The light shines in darkness, and the darkness has not overcome it.
There was a man sent from God, whose name was John. He came for testimony, to bear witness to the light, that all might believe through Him. He was not the Light, but came to bear witness to the light. The true light that enlightens every man was coming into the world. He was in the world, and the world was made through Him and the world knew him not. He came unto his own, and those who were his own received him not. But to all who received him, who believed in his name, he gave power to become children of God; Who were born, not of blood

*nor of the will of the flesh nor the will of Man, but of God And
the word became flesh and dwelt among us, full of grace and
truth; we have beheld his glory, glory as of the only Son of the
Father.*

John 1: 1–14

*Now when they heard this, they were cut to the heart, and said
to Peter and the rest of the apostles, "Brethren, what shall we
do?" And Peter said to them, "Repent, be baptized in the Name
of Jesus Christ for the forgiveness of your sins and you will receive the gift of the Holy Spirit."*

Acts 2:37–38 RSV

*You know about Jesus of Nazareth, how God anointed him with
the Holy Spirit and with power, He went about doing good and
healing all who were oppressed by the devil for God was with
Him. And we can bear witness to all that He did in the Jewish
countryside and in Jerusalem. He was put to death by hanging
on a gibbet: but God raised Him to life on the third day, and allowed Him to appear not to the whole people, but to witnesses
whom God has chosen in advance to us, who ate and drank
with Him after He rose from the dead. He commanded us to
proclaim Him to the people, and affirm that He is the one who
has been designated by God as judge of the living and the
dead. It is to Him that all prophets testify declaring that everyone who trusts in Him receives forgiveness of sins through His
name.*

Acts 10:30–43.

These testimonies of Jesus found in scripture enrich the per-
ception of Him, but they do not totally define Him. In the black
church we believe the Bible, but we believe also the God of the
Bible. Although the Bible is the authoritative voice of the black
church, what we read about does not totally define who God is.
Preaching and scriptures are not the only authoritative sources
in the black church.

Spirituals are important in understanding hospitality as a norm for moral discourse. Black spirituals have guided the black church historically and provided hope against the destructive force of oppression. E. Hammond Oglesby says "The black spirituals contain ethical content and valuable insight into the wellspring of human existence."[14] The spirituals constitute a unique moral language, a peculiar pattern of communication to those experiencing oppression in their immediate situation. Oglesby says, "Housed implicitly in the Black Spirituals are three major factors for us to consider:"

1. A concern for freedom in earthly life.
2. Songs expressing moral admonition and guidance for human conduct.
3. Songs of aspiration expressing essentially the ethic of hope.

In unpacking these three tenets, Oglesby has this to say: "First, the spirituals gave moral direction in what seemingly may be described as a 'directionless world' where the white man called all of the shots."[15] "That the Spirituals provided a kind of vision, a world of the soul that could not be managed or manipulated by the white man." He calls this a normative light, which enabled the oppressed and alienated black man to literally walk through the wilderness of slavery and not get irrationally disturbed. Worth noting is the fact that the slaves, those who were oppressed, loved life itself. Their problems in life consisted of the situation and circumstances of the oppression in which they found themselves. Succinctly put, their problem was not with God; they had a profound sense of God, and their faith in God was unmovable.

However, they had a fundamental problem with their slave-master and the dehumanizing system of oppression. Having the ability to sing under these circumstances is remarkable. There was another group of people, "Israel," in like circumstance, "exile," who could not sing. This truth is depicted in: Psalm 137:

> *By the rivers of Babylon, there we sat down and wept when we remembered Zion. On the willows in the midst of it we hung our lyres. For there our captors required of us songs, and our tormentors mirth, saying. Sing us one of the Songs of Zion. How can we sing the Lord's song in a foreign Land?*

With a heavy heart, in a strange land, songs are not easy to come by. However, in contrast, black people in these conditions of exile, could not keep from singing as a way of demonstrating their persuasion of hope. Oglesby reflected on songs like:

> *Oh, walk togedder children,*
> *Don't yer get weary*
> *Oh, walk togedder children*
> *Don't yer get weary*
> *Oh, walk togedder children*
> *Don't yer get weary*
> *Dere a Great Camp meeting*
> *In de Promised Land!*

This spiritual speaks of life. It affirms the hope of unity and solidarity of looking together and sharing the joy of "the Promised Land."

Not shrinking from their condition of exile, their creative ingenuity was expressed in songs like:

> *We are climbing Jacob's ladder*
> *We are climbing Jacob's ladder*
> *We are climbing Jacob's ladder*
> *Soldiers of the Cross*
>
> *Every round goes higher, higher*
> *Every round goes higher, higher*

> *Every round goes higher, higher*
> *Soldiers of the Cross*
>
> *Sinner, do you love my Jesus?*
> *Sinner, do you love my Jesus?*
> *Sinner, do you love my Jesus?*
> *Soldiers of the Cross.*
>
> *If you love Him why not serve Him?*
> *If you love Him why not serve Him?*
> *If you love Him why not serve Him?*
> *Soldiers of the Cross.*

While Israel found it hard to sing the Psalms, black folks found it the only thing to do. And even if the slave owners took the song from their lips, they had music in their heads and hearts to guide them and help make their situation more tolerable.

Secondly, Oglesby suggests that the measure of freedom anticipated by the oppressed black man under the yoke of slavery, was often contemplated in proportion to, or in relationship to the probability of death in one's attempt to struggle for freedom.

What he says can be summed up in this classical black spiritual,

> *Oh Freedom! Oh Freedom*
> *Oh Freedom! I love thee*
> *And before I'll be a slave*
> *I'll be buried in my grave*
> *And go home to my Lord and be Free.*

The spiritual expresses, in essence, that death in some instances does not have to be looked at as an enemy, but as a friend. In the slave condition—without honor and dignity,

without a sense of worth or human value—death for the sake
of freedom, was not a bad option, but could be looked at as an
honoring of freedom.

Thirdly, Oglesby says, that the black slave, through the spirituals, expressed an ethic of hope. This meant that they knew,
existentially speaking, that this world was not their home.
They had their hearts and minds set on "lofty heights," on
higher goals and on "heavenly places." This expressed both
transcendent points of reference and a passionate concern for
moral freedom through persistent struggle in this world. To illustrate this merger, the words of this spiritual are offered up as
a sacrifice:

> *Don't let nobody turn you around,*
> *turn you around, turn you around*
> *turn you around. Don't let nobody*
> *turn you around. You gotta keep on*
> *walking up the King's highway.*

It is as if they were saying in their singing that their real meaning as human beings and their real purpose in life was not to be
found in their present location of oppression, but in a place
where the first and last would be treated the same.

Although there has been a revolution of sorts in the black
experience as it relates to music (with gospel music being
more prevalent and contemporary), guided by pioneers such
as Thomas A. Dorsey, James Cleveland, Dorothy Norwood
and others, I agree with the assessment of Enoch Oglesby,
"that the Spirituals express the conviction and foundational
belief that the Promised Land will be ascertained because God
is on the side of the oppressed. That God has His finger in the
plan of liberation."[16] That God is against any form of oppression, therefore the claim is made that God is on the side of the
oppressed.

Historically, the preached word, the Bible, spirituals and the community are all important in strengthening the inner life of the believer for the outer work that they will do in the church. These four moral norms are the shaping principles used to enhance the Black church as an agent of action, and to keep in focus hospitality as a form of obligation and moral responsibility.

After considering the moral norms that have guided the black church historically, let us now turn our attention to hospitality as a moral obligation in the context of the Shalom Church.

Hospitality is a pro-formative term. It is an act of kindness demonstrated to "the other." These acts of kindness should normally function without the thought of reciprocation. However, there is one reciprocating occurrence of hospitality because each of us at some point in our lives find ourselves being "the other," needing to be shown some hospitality. When hospitality is extended it would be destructive to the moral and ethical order of things to think that a sense of gratitude and obligation would not emerge. If it does not, then the person has taken the position of one who is self-sufficient and autonomous. For instance, as people of faith we became *dependent upon* and *grateful for* the provision the Creator has made for us. The sun, the seasons, the rain, the water, the night, day, life, peace, joy, family, etc., all yield a response of gratitude.

However, these things also yield a sense of obligation to do and to share that which has been received. Therefore, one's gratitude to the Creator can best be seen in one's obligation to "the creature," and "the other." James M. Gustafson writes in *Ethics from a Theocentric Perspective* that:

"Religion is grounded in human experience. Theology is not a reflection upon something supernatural, as if we could reflect on something that is not in any way related to human experience. But religion is grounded in the experience of 'others' of nature, of human communities, of human cultures, provides myths, symbols, and analogies which interpret the meaning and significance of various aspects of the human experience in the light of convictions that life is not a human creation, that its destiny is not fully in human control, that there are requirements of human action and relations that have to be met for the sake of survival and flourishing and that absolute fatedness is not the human lot."[17]

In essence, all of life is interrelated and interconnected and because of that, there needs to remain an obligation and sensitivity to otherness. In the context of Shalom Church, the question of otherness is most important. The Shalom Church is located in Berkeley, Missouri. Surrounded by poverty, crime, and gangs—a stereotypically *urban setting*, the "other" in this community is viewed as very dangerous. How do upwardly mobile people, such as those at Shalom Church, become host to such "dangerous others" who may not understand hospitality as a deliberate practice of ministry, but see it rather as in invasion of their comfortable tribal space? There are several avenues that should be considered in addressing these concerns.

Where the gift of hospitality is practiced at the Shalom Church, the practice must not be an isolated incident of kindness. The gift must edify congregational life, and to a larger degree, speak to the hostilities while offering hospitality to the community in which the church finds itself. This gift should not only be recognized and celebrated, but also grounded in the gospel of Jesus Christ, the ecclesiological practice of the congregation. Gospel oriented hospitality will always be more interested in the needs of the *guest* than those of the *host*. For instance, consider the parables that Jesus told to emphasize the value in human personality and creating space where the other is given consideration.

And behold, a lawyer stood up to put him to the test saying, "Teacher, what shall I do to inherit eternal life?" He said to

him, "What is written in the law? How do you read? And he answered, you shall love the Lord your God with all your heart, and with all your soul, and with all your strength, and with all your mind; and your neighbor as yourself. And He said to him, you have answered right; do this and you will live. But he, desiring to justify himself, he said to Jesus, "And who is my neighbor?" Jesus replied and said, "A man was going down from Jerusalem to Jericho, And fell among robbers, and they stripped him and beat him, and went away leaving him half-dead. Now by chance a priest was going down on that road, and when he saw him, he passed by on the other side. So likewise a Levite also when he came to the place and saw him, passed by on the other side. But a Samaritan, as he journeyed, came to where he was and when he saw him he had compassion, And he went to him and bandaged up his wounds, pouring on oil and wine; then he set Him on his own beast, and brought him to an inn and took care of him. And the next day he took out two denarii and gave them to the innkeeper, saying, "Take care of him; whatever more you spend, I will repay you when I come back." Which of these three do you think proved to be a neighbor to the man who fell into the robber's hands?
Luke 10:25–38

I have discovered that the motive for which we ask the question is just as important as the answer. For instance, the lawyer wanted to justify himself by narrowing this concept that included the few and not the many. The lawyer was more interested in theological speculation than in practical application. In this parable Jesus opens up the possibilities of where and how we meet our neighbor. Our neighbor is the one who is immediately before us. In the parable the neighbor is avoided in the name of religion. Religious business often triumphs over human need. When law comes before love; ritualism, institutionalism and moralism will prevail. However, when love is at the core of one's essence while following Jesus, one cannot help but stop and respond to the human hurt. Lastly, in the parable, help comes from unlikely sources, that is, the Samaritan. The Samaritan went out of his way to help this man. He was not willing to turn this man's future over to someone else. Instead, he took the responsibility himself. Perhaps he looked at the man and saw the history of his own mistreatment, and responded faithfully by helping the interpreter to retain an active imagination in the quest for understanding. It is Thomas Ogletree who, in the book *Hospitality to the Stranger*, uses hospitality as a metaphor for understanding moral life.

Ogletree says that the central thrust of the metaphor of hospitality is to break the preoccupation of ethical theory with perceptions and reasoning stemming from a given actor's own vantage point of the world. It is to accomplish in ethics what the parables accomplished in Jesus, a realignment of one's perspective of the world. For instance, Ogletree says, "to offer hospitality to a stranger is to welcome something new, unfamiliar, and unknown into our life-world."[18] He goes on to say that hospitality in its metaphorical usage, is a way to understand that moral obligation does not simply render to literal instances of interaction with persons from society and cultures other than our own. It suggests attention to "otherness" in its many expressions. Hospitality to the stranger is a metaphor, for the moral life has a dimension that includes "otherness." It is, in a practical sense, "other," the personal "other" that we come to know ethically, morally, religiously and responsibly. It is the "other" addressing me, who alone can call into question my egotism, moving me to live by and toward a new orientation that includes "otherness."

Hospitality as a deliberate practice of ministry of the Shalom Church, in the Berkeley community, where there is the typical "urban" setting is to unconditionally acknowledge the "other" who is very much like ourselves. This should not be some sentimental arrangement to win the stranger to church membership (although hospitality is a great tool for evangelism). Instead, it is a de-centering of ourselves so that the stranger/other can have a sense of "at homeness" as he/she is being transformed from stranger to host and we are being transformed from host to stranger/other. "Hospitality to the stranger," says Ogletree, "points toward an ongoing dialectic of host and stranger."[19] I can have my world in a moral way only as I learn to relate it positively to the contrasting world of others.

The reality of the Berkeley community was as it is now, when we moved into the building, which houses our congregation. This community already had an on-going historical narrative. This is to suggest that Shalom Church could have been viewed by the community's lens, as the dangerous stranger in their presence. What is more agonizing and incriminating is that the forms of hospitality extended from the community to us may have been grossly overlooked. After all, we are the church, the institution with the history and tradition and, of course, the place that holds all of the advantages in forming a relationship. The "other" in this community perhaps was not seen as an equal in the distribution of what could be offered. However, when we consider that we have had the freedom to move in and out of this community unharmed, this is a form of hospitality and an act of pure grace. To further illustrate, let me share this experience.

As I was leaving church late on a Saturday afternoon, I was approached by three young men (who appeared to want to cause me some discomfort). As I started to my car, much to my surprise, one of the young men called my name. I immediately (in my mind) took a defensive attitude and I responded, loud and forcefully, not knowing what to expect. His response will live with me for the rest of my life as an example of the dialectic of host/stranger. He said, "We have fried some fish and noticed that you have been here all day. If you are hungry we can bring you something to eat." "We can bring you something to eat."

That's amazing, that "the other" who appeared to be disadvantaged" said to me, the holder of the gifts, "there is something we can do for you."

What this means in the context of our every day shared experience is that the Shalom Church, with the gift of hospitality, must also learn to receive the act of hospitality. To hear the historical narrative of the other is then to know that we don't have power over, but power with those who are our neighbors.

What it means to experience hospitality as a *gift received* instead of a gift shared is to understand Henri Nouwen's paradoxical assessment of "poverty making a good host."[20] If Thomas Ogletree uses hospitality as a metaphor for moral understanding, then Henri Nouwen uses hospitality as a way of developing spiritually. Nouwen suggests in *Reaching Out: Three Movements of the Spiritual Life* that once we have found the center of our life in our own heart and have accepted our aloneness, not as a fate but as a vocation, we are able to offer freedom to others. Once we have given up our desire to be fully fulfilled, we can offer emptiness to others. Once we have become poor, we can be a good host." This is the paradox of hospitality because a good host is full of that which they willingly want to impart to the stranger. However, spiritually speaking, with the movement of Nouwen, there must be a poverty of one's inner disposition that would make them responsibly a good host. Nouwen says, "Poverty takes away our defenses and converts our enemies to friends" and "that we can only perceive the stranger as an enemy as long as we have something to defend."[21]

In developing this understanding of hospitality as a spiritual discipline and the poverty that is necessary for embracing this discipline, Nouwen went on to name where this poverty is to be evident; in mind and in heart.

With the poverty of mind there is an openness to receive new knowledge, new opportunities, new relationships. Nouwen says,

"Someone who is filled with ideas, concepts, opinions, and convictions cannot be a good host. There is no inner space to listen, no openness to discover the gift of the other."[22] They, in fact, know it all; therefore there is no exchange. With every new encounter there is something to be learned because there is something to be shared. Strangers have stories to tell which we have never heard before; stories which can redirect our vision and stimulate our imaginations. Their stories may even be threatening, but not necessarily so, but if so, know that with any exchange there is a possibility of change. That is what the poverty of mind seeks to do, change us. We are becoming ignorant for the sake of a greater learning experience that would make us more hospitable.

A good host, according to Nouwen, not only has to be poor in mind but also poor in heart. The heart has to be emptied of all fears that create distance. When our hearts are filled with prejudices, worries, jealousies, there is no room for the stranger.

Strange as it may seem, hospitality, as a spiritual discipline, requires that we become emptied before we find fulfillment. In a world that wants to operate on full, the core of the Christian message is found in our being weak and empty. Consider this Philippianic passage:

> *Who, though he was in the form of God, did not count equality with God a thing to be grasped, But emptied himself, taking the form of a servant, being born in the likeness of men. And being found in human form he humbled Himself and became obedient unto death, even death on a cross.*
>
> Philippians 2:6–8

It is abundantly clear that Shalom Church, as well as every faith-based institution operating from a biblical perspective, is to extend hospitality to all strangers. How easy it is to welcome the well-dressed, the upwardly mobile, those who have something we think might benefit us. But how about the many other strangers God sends our way? What about the elderly, the physically or mentally challenged, the unwed couple (living together), the couple recently married who have fallen on hard times, the homosexual and the lesbian, the person with AIDS, the person recently released from prison, the white collar criminal recently indicted? How will we welcome these persons?

It will not happen unless one deliberately acknowledges that hospitality to the stranger is a moral obligation. For the Shalom Church, it has to be embedded in our theological understanding of who we are.

Hospitality is a deliberative practice. This norm must be taught in the church from a moral perspective and as a spiritual discipline. We shall now turn our attention to the question of ecclesiology and mission in the context of our public life.

Chapter III

Ecclesiology and Mission: Hospitality as a Public Way of Life

Hospitality as ministerial practice and a public way of life must be grounded in the gospel of Jesus Christ. In this chapter, with the focus on ecclesiology and mission, I will consider the new commandment Jesus gives in the gospel as a way of honoring the poor and oppressed that creates ways of offering hospitality as a public way of life. I will also consider the ecclesiological practice of the Lord's Supper as a sacramental sign that the church grapples with in trying to understand the many ways it encounters the stranger in their midst. It will be important for me to include the black church historically as a stranger in the world confronting hostilities for the sake of hospitality. Lastly, there will be reflections on how this practice enables the Shalom Church to participate in the activity of God in the world.

The church can never understand itself in isolation; it can only understand its roles and functions, its meaning and mission in relationship to others. Simply put, without Christ there is no church, without Christ there is no mission for the church. Christ's mission is not because of the church; the church has a mission because of Christ. The church has no light in and of itself. The light that is reflected from the face of the church is

Christ. Therefore, the first word that the church seeks should not be about itself, but Christ. It is the ultimate aim of the church's witness in the world to bring about transformation where it exists. Moreover, in any effort that the church undertakes, whether it is the area of stewardship, evangelism, mission and or social justice, the ultimate aim is to make known the rule of God through the person of Jesus Christ. This is no less true of how one comes to understand hospitality as a practice of ministry that shapes persons for their everyday existence in the world.

Every day we are overwhelmed with visible reminders of the vastness of human hurts and fragmented lives. Our cities are saturated with crime and violence, despair and hopelessness. The local news seems to focus on these tragedies and out of the immensity of what is being watched, there develops a degree of indifference and insensitivity. If we are not careful, we might fall into the trap of blaming the victims for their plight in life instead of a system that does not work for those who are disconnected. Hospitality, as an ecclesiological practice and a public way of life seeks to find commonality with the woefully disconnected "other," to develop a relationship where they are perceived as equals.

Thomas Ogletree says, "Regard for the stranger in their vulnerability and delight in their novel offerings presupposes that we perceive them as equals; as persons who share our common humanity in its myriad variation."[23] However, even with this truth, as Christians, we declare that we order our lives based on God's revelation in the scripture, rather than mere emotional response. It is not sufficient to bring Christians into action, no matter how dire the need. *Whether* we should act, or *how* we should act, depends upon that which has been assigned our hands through the gospel of Jesus Christ. The church is not in the world looking for something to do, some cause to champion, some issue to rally around. The church has been given its orders, how it should live as a hospitable community in the world. The church has a moral and biblical obligation associated with hospitality.

God's people then, are called to be imitators of God. We have been recipients of God's grace and care. In turn, we are to act as God Himself would mercifully act toward those who are aliens and strangers. Jesus said,

> *Go therefore, and make disciples of all nations, baptizing them in the name of the Father and the Son, and the Holy Spirit. Teaching them to observe all that I commanded you; and lo, I am with you always, even to the end of the age.*
>
> Matthew 28:19–20

The disciples of Jesus Christ are to *make* disciples. Disciples are made by sharing with all people the teachings of Jesus so that His church would be rooted in nothing but that which they received from Him. Even before the command and commissioning of Matthew 28, the disciples were instructed to remain sensitive to those who were out of the social loop—the blind, lame, the poor—consider them. The first blessing that Jesus announced in the Sermon on the Mount was for the poor in spirit (Matthew 5:3). In His inaugural speech, that was in the tradition of Deutero Isaiah, and that included humanity's oppressed, He made clear the focus of His mission and ministry. It is the poor, the oppressed, the blind, the socially dysfunctional that become the focus of the gospel, creating an alternative for this portion of humanity that has been excluded. The message is that God is with us in Jesus Christ, and all of what has been announced will be ushered in by Jesus Himself. This speech defined for disciples of every generation that same focus, when He said:

> *And there was given to him the book of the prophet Isaiah. He opened the book and found the place where it was written,*

"The Spirit of the Lord is upon me because he has anointed me to preach good news to the poor. He has sent me to proclaim release to the captives and recovering sight to the blind, to set at liberty those who are oppressed to proclaim the acceptable year of the Lord." And he closed the book and gave it back to the attendant, and sat down; and the eyes of all in the synagogue were fixed on him and he began to say to them, "Today this scripture has been fulfilled in your hearing."

Luke 4:1721 (RSV)

It is the gospel of Jesus Christ that addresses these categories of poverty for the sake of liberation and ultimately turning these hostilities into lives that offer hospitality. Now, for the socially poor, the message of Jesus is good news. However, for others, His message presents a moral challenge.

This message begins with the poor and ends with liberation for all who will hear and follow. Now, while mentioning the poor, one cannot assume that this is the class item "poor" that is often imagined when we hear this word. For instance, we know there are the economic, social or physical poor. These are they who Jesus defines as the biblical poor. However, there are also the psychological, moral and religious poor, in short, those who are poor and do not know they're poor. They are the poor in spirit. In any event, the message of liberation is to be preached to all of the poor; those who have *endured* acts of violence and injustice without being able to defend themselves, and the poor who *inflict* this kind of violence. The poor who are always at the mercy of others, living with *empty* and *open* hands, as well as the poor who live with tightly clenched hands, depending on no one, nor being able to respond to anyone. They will be able to give from the abundance of their resources, sharing with others, becoming poor so that they will truly be rich. The richness of our existence is found in an ability to embrace the "*other*," even when the "*other*" can give nothing in return. The rich will only be truly rich when they recognize their own poverty.

Jesus tells this story which speaks with clarity about how we are to respond to the poor in our midst. Before offering interpretation to these verses, it is David E. Holwerda in *Jesus and Israel: One Covenant or Two?* who lifts several questions about law and the age of fulfillment. He asked, "If the new era has already dawned, can the law of the old era still survive? Or, what happens to the law of the Old Testament when the eschatological light shines in the darkness?"[24] The coming of Jesus Christ created a significant challenge to understanding the Old Testament law. Some Christian traditions believe that the law has come to an end, and no longer has anything to do with the Christian believer. Others believe that we are free from the law, but yet the life of the Christian is characterized by making a connection with the law.

As he was setting out on a journey, a man ran up to Him and knelt before Him, and asked Him, Good Teacher, "What shall I do to inherit eternal Life?" And Jesus said to him, "Why do you call me good? No one is good but God alone. You know the commandments, Do not murder, Do not commit adultery, Do not steal, Do not bear false witness, Do not defraud, Honor your father and mother. And he said to him, Teacher, I have kept all these things from my youth up. Looking at him, Jesus felt a love for him and said to him, One thing you lack, go and sell all you possess and give to the poor, and you will have treasure in heaven, and come follow me. But at these words he was saddened, and went away grieving for he was one who owned much property. And Jesus looked around and said to His disciples, how hard it will be for those who are wealthy to enter the kingdom of God.

Mark 10:17-23

In the young ruler's request for eternal life, it is love for the neighbor as a way of loving oneself that really moves toward a clearer understanding of the new commandment.

The new commandment Jesus gives centers on the inclusion of the poor. "Sell what you have and give to the poor, and you will have treasure in heaven, and come follow me" (Mark 10:21). What Jesus attempts to do is to give the young ruler an opportunity to practice righteousness that goes beyond the law by practicing compassion and hospitality to the poor. Yet, even with his possessions, the challenging invitation that Jesus gives is simply to do more with your resources than to keep them for yourself. Consider the poor and find favor with God. Verse 22 reads, "But at these words, he was saddened, and went away grieving, for he was one who owned much property."

David Holwerda says, "the commandment of Jesus to follow Him is a climactic demand that goes well beyond an Old Testament requirement. In this story the demand for lawfulness ends with a demand for discipleship. Also this walk that disciples are to have with Jesus requires a love for one's neighbor and a sharing of God's gifts with the poor."[25] Eternal life is not to be a possession like the many other possessions that persons hold onto while trying to follow Jesus.

Consequently, when the rich young man affirms that he has kept all the laws, he really demonstrates how little he understood the law requirement of Jesus. When Jesus instructs the man to sell what he has and give to the poor, Jesus takes the man beyond the place he is willing to go. Although the new command is radical, it contains what true righteousness is about. Being perfect before God is not solely a matter of keeping the law, but it is also a matter of being perfect in one's relationship with other people. An inability to recognize one's own poverty (as was the case of the young ruler) may also prevent such persons from seeing Jesus Christ and understanding

His vision for the world. That vision includes the *disconnected* in our world that the church must address using the practice of hospitality. The new commandment Jesus gives in the gospel is a way of honoring the poor and oppressed that creates ways of offering hospitality as a public way of life.

Not only is there to be a certain equality that is established with the poor, but also a commonality that looks beyond the world schemes. Therefore, another ecclesiological practice that honors hospitality as a way of public life is the Lord's Supper. I will consider the ecclesiological practice of the Lord's Supper as a sacramental sign that the church grapples with in trying to understand the many ways it encounters the strangers in their midst. It is at the table that persons participate with God in celebrating what God has done through Jesus Christ. There is participation with others who are a part of God's family, and a participation of what God is doing in the world. The Christian life finds its center, its point of concentration at the table; without it, the Christian life is simply unthinkable.

Although referred to by several other names such as "Communion," "The Love Meal" and "Eucharist," I will be referring to it in this context as "The Lord's Supper." Each has a common ecclesiological foundation that is open for the peace and righteousness of God's presence in the world. Somehow, God is not satisfied *in* the world or *with* the world until all have eaten.

On the Sunday we observe the Lord's Supper at the Shalom Church, I stand before the table of God's people and speak these words:

For I received from the Lord what I also delivered to you that the Lord Jesus in the night in which He was betrayed took bread And when he had given thanks, He broke it and said, "This is My body which is broken for you: do this in remembrance of Me!" In the same way also the cup, after supper, saying, "This cup is the new covenant in my blood. Do this, As often as you drink it, in remembrance of me For as often as you eat this bread and drink the cup you proclaim the Lord's death until He comes."

I Corinthians 11:23–26

After I recited these things, I would ask, "Has everyone been served?" I would wait a few seconds that somehow seemed like an eternity and I'd ask the question again, "Has everyone been served?" After realizing that everyone in the sanctuary had been served, we then would move to eat together, and drink together, properly finalizing the meal. However, it is only gradually that we came to hear and better understand the question at the table, "Has everyone been served?" The question echoes beyond the walls of the sanctuary, out into the world of many human hurts and hungers. The Lord's Supper is not finished until everyone has been served.

Hospitality, as an ecclesiological practice that is nurtured and informed at the Lord's Supper table, will seek to serve the world by offering the world Jesus Christ, Who is the bread of life, and discovered by sharing the sacrament of oneness with the world.

In many ways, the ritual of the Lord's Supper at the Shalom Church has been rightly instituted. However, beyond the ritual of the formative experience, the hope is to see the Lord's Supper as the theological instrument, which fashions hospitality as a practice in the world. The Lord's Supper gives the church a sacramental identity. The Lord's Supper is the sacrament in the church that remembers the liberating suffering of Christ, His redeeming future and glory. In this meal, His past and future are simultaneously made present. In His presence, the church is freed from the powers of the world that lead to sin and separation. The Lord's Supper is for all of God's people, where God gives an open invitation to come and share the meal.

However, Christ is above His church and can call into question any activity that the church practices that does not honor Him.

When I was younger, I experienced an awareness of what the table meant. The leadership of our local congregation practiced a kind of moral legalism that accompanied the meal. The leaders required a certain worthiness to qualify people for a place at the table. Even in my first pastorate, I sensed the same moral necessity was embedded into the minds of those whom I was called to serve. If by chance, when inventorying their personal practice as a Christian, there was something that was considered a sin that they had committed, they would be refused entry to the table. Most of this I learned as a result of reading or misreading:

> *Whoever, therefore, eats the bread or drinks the cup of the Lord in an unworthy manner, will be guilty of profaning the body and the blood of the Lord*
>
> I Corinthians 11:27

What I have discovered in unpacking this practice was the word "unworthy." Many thought that unworthy behavior disqualified them from accepting this open invitation from the Lord Jesus, who said, "Do this in remembrance of Me." What I also discovered in the process of unpacking this practice was that the entire theological understanding of what it meant to be a servant of Jesus Christ in the world was centered in a kind of legal *"moralism"* that not only spoiled the meal, but created divisions and hostilities in attempting to live up to this responsibility. The Lord's Supper is a sign of Christ's fellowship that unites and allows for commonality that creates hospitality among those who have been called by Him, and who seek to live out their call as a public way of life.

I use the term "Lord's Supper" to talk about the table as a way to understand the task of being in the Lord's service and in fellowship with others and also as a way to be hospitable in a world that is broken and fragmented needing to be served the bread of life. Henri J. Nouwen provides further clarity when describing hospitality as an ecclesiological practice by using the word "Eucharist," which means literally "thanksgiving." A Eucharistic life is lived in gratitude. Nouwen, in his book *With Burning Hearts*, takes us on a five-step journey using the Emmaus Road narrative to demonstrate the moves from resentment to gratitude. Nouwen says, "The Emmaus Road story, which is the story of two friends walking, shows that gratitude is not an obvious attitude toward life. Gratitude needs to be discovered and lived with greater inner attentiveness. The Eucharist celebration keeps inviting us to that attitude of being grateful."[26] However, it is only when we recognize the rich network of connections between the Eucharist that we become worldly and our lives Eucharistic. This is certainly in connection with how the stranger is received.

In the gospel of Luke, Chapter 24:13-32, the stranger becomes the guiding force to help us see anew.

The encounter becomes interesting when Jesus, the stranger joins them on the Emmaus Road in their pain, and *in* their pain, they listen to this stranger explain the scripture to them. As they listen, their hurt turns to hope. Nouwen suggests the word of the Eucharist makes us part of the great story of salvation. Our little stories are lifted up into God's great story and they're given their unique place. The word lifts us up and makes us see that our daily, ordinary lives are, in fact, sacred lives that play a necessary role in the fulfillment of God's promise. What is seen is that accepting the stranger and what the stranger has to offer can provide for us an avenue of looking at the world that we never dreamed possible. Parker Palmer says, "The function of the stranger in our lives is grounded in a simple fact: Truth is a very large matter that requires various angles of vision to be seen in the round. It is not that our view is always wrong, and the stranger is always right, but simply that the stranger's view is always different, giving us an opportunity to look anew at familiar things." As the two travelers pressed the stranger to stay with them, they are, in essence, inviting him to lay aside his strangeness and become a friend. This is what true hospitality is all about, that is offering the stranger, not only space, but a place to be himself. Nouwen goes on to say further that, "the table is a place of intimacy. The table is a place where we discover each other." There is much that goes into this discovery, however, this is not always the case in dealing with the stranger in our midst.

Parker Palmer, in *The Company of Strangers* writes: "Openness to the stranger, and to letting the stranger be, is resisted by the basic dynamics of community formation."[27] An intimate community is formed by an act of exclusion, "we" are in and "they" are out. The very fact that a group of people have a sense of community with one another suggests that they have drawn a boundary around themselves, that they see themselves as different from the surrounding world. The stranger threatens the foundations of such a community by blurring the boundary; the stranger must either be kept out or made to become like the community. However, when a community's identity is being shaped by the gospel of Jesus Christ, and that community sees and understands the table as a sign of fellowship with Him and commonality with the other, the stranger can be embraced with understanding. This is the moral foundation of hospitality that is strengthened at the Lord's Supper table.

The word "intimacy," like hospitality, perhaps denotes some flowery sentimental arrangement of being in relationship with the other. However, intimacy in terms of discovery at the table, uncovers the real truth of one's identity. The table is the place of both laughter and tears, togetherness and separation, hospitality and hostilities. It's the place where jealousies surface,

accusations are made and the pain of betrayal is felt. Certainly
this is a dimension of scriptural story.

> *When it was evening he sat at table with the twelve disciples;*
> *and as they were eating, he said, "Truly, I say to you, one of*
> *you will betray me." And they were sorrowful and began to say*
> *to him one after another, "Is it I, Lord?" He answered, "He*
> *who has dipped his hand in the dish with me will betray me."*
> Matthew 26:20-23

There never seemed to have been a time in our house when
the whole family came together to celebrate something (birth-
day, graduation, birth or even death), when somebody did not
get their feelings hurt. Tension filled the air about some old ri-
valry or misunderstanding. However, reflecting upon those
times, no matter how thick the tension, no matter how obvious
the pain, to come to the table and eat the food that was prepared, invited a way of bonding that enabled family to work
through some very emotional issues. In like manner, the Lord's
Supper table is not simply the place where hospitality to the
stranger is offered, but friends around the table work through
hostilities toward reconciliation.

To further illustrate the example of the table being a place of
intimacy and identity shaping, Jesus addresses the company of
the stranger from within using the tools of privacy and intimacy. The biblical vision invites us to give up ourselves to the
point of opening ourselves to the perspective of the stranger.

During supper, "the devil having already put into the heart
of Judas Iscariot, the Son of Simon to betray Him."

> *Jesus knowing that the Father had given all things into his*
> *hands, and that he had come from God and was going to God,*
> *rose from supper, laid aside His garments, and girded himself*
> *with a towel. Then He poured water into a basin, and began to*
> *wash the disciples' feet, and to wipe them with the towel with*

which He was girded. He came to Simon Peter; and Peter said to him, "Lord, do you wash my feet?" Jesus answered him, "What I am doing you do not know now but . . . If I do not wash you, you have no part of me." Simon Peter said to him afterward "You will understand." Peter said to him, "You will never wash my feet." Jesus answered him, "Lord, not only my feet but also my hands and my head! Jesus said to him, "He who has bathed does not need to wash, except for his feet, but he is clean all over; and you are clean, but not every one of you. For He knew who was to betray him; that was why He said, "You are not all clean." When He had washed their feet, and taken His garments, and resumed His place, He said to them, "Do you know what I have done to you?" You call me Teacher and Lord; and you are right, for so I am.

John 13:3-14

There is at the table with Jesus during this time a stranger who is very dangerous. However, the act of intimacy, using the tools of hospitality and privacy, elevates and transforms the stranger from within to a friend. That willingness is what allows us to share meaning as well as to perceive difference. Patrick R. Keifert in *Welcoming the Stranger* states, "The biblical vision of intimacy stands in sharp contrast to the ideology of intimacy at the social and psychological level. Rather than projecting the private onto the public, it opens the door for the stranger (even the stranger from within). The biblical vision affirms public interaction through the command of hospitality to the stranger."[28] Hospitality to the stranger from a biblical perspective implies wisdom, love, and justice, as opposed to other ideologies that might suggest warmth, familiarity and intimacy. Patrick Keifert suggests that the impersonal justice and love required by biblical command is not impersonal in the sense of being unkind, unloving, or unfeeling, but it specifically does not depend upon a personal history or ties between those interacting in the public, the exchange of one's most intimate thoughts and feelings, or the physical intimacy common among family and friends. It treats interaction without a demand for friendship or virtue.

For hospitality to become an ecclesiological practice of ministry and a public way of life, as welcoming and interacting with the stranger, whether that stranger be a public wanderer or personal friend, there are several perspectives that need to be considered: When we speak of being brothers and sisters, we are speaking about being united with Christ through the power of the Holy Spirit and fellowship at the Lord's table. Also, what we enjoy as a fellowshipping people is not based upon our intimacy, but on Christ through the intimacy of word and sacrament. While using the imagery of the family, there is no family without encounters of both joy and pain. Remember that all people are God's children and potentially our brothers and sisters in Christ.

I will now look at the black church, which has historically been a stranger in the world confronting hostilities for the sake of hospitality. We have talked about the Emmaus Road as a way of being confronted by the stranger. The Emmaus Road image provides a way for me to address the issues of the black church as a stranger joining the other establishments in history for the sake of becoming a part of the shared process. The metaphor that will be important is that of "journey." The black church confronts the historical establishments in what I perceive to be an Emmaus Road encounter.

We are on our own Emmaus Road being confronted by the stranger. If hospitality is to be an ecclesiological practice of ministry and the public way of life, how we treat the stranger in our presence is of utmost importance. Remember the stranger carries with them blessings that will not be revealed if the stranger is not embraced. Such a stranger that emerged and attempted to give definition and clarity to the injustices that were being perpetrated on them in North America was the black church. It is important to remember that any discussion of black existence in American society must include a discussion of the black church. The black church is the primary institution in the black community. It is its center. It is often hard to distinguish between the "black church" and the "black community" because they are so intrinsically tied together. The black church that emerged on the Emmaus Road journey as the stranger in the presence of the white mainline church and other social institutions did not find hospitality, but instead resistance and hostility. There was, beyond her wall, an existing world that was segregated, hostile and fragmented. The black church's involvement in the world exists not for her own sake, but to make the world better for all people. The black church was never privileged to be a part of the larger partnership of any mainline white churches or the wider public, thus moving them to monitor their own existence.

E. Franklin Frazier, while talking about the black church, has called her genesis "The Invisible Institution."[29] This institution called "invisible" had, as its important figure, the preacher who was both spiritual guide and educator. Even in the invisible institution, an ecclesiology of spiritual nurturing, education and survival emerged. The invisible institution for black folks was the only outlet that slaves exercised as a measure of freedom. Thus, religion became the only institutional area that permitted blacks to expand. The church was the nurturing ground for hopeful possibilities. It was their place of refuge, their place of hospitality in an oppressive hostile world. Here, I have been defining hospitality in its interior dynamics and as a place for strangers, who have not been received, developing means to take care of themselves.

As time passed, there was a merger of the invisible institution (black church) and the Institutional Church. The invisible institution, which had taken away the black slaves, and the visible institutional church which had grown up among the blacks that were free before the Civil War, provided a rapid growth in size and the ability to organize toward the acceptable mainstream. Peter Paris, stated, "The growth of the black church is both significant and inspirational. In its history lie the stories of countless men and women, often slaves and runaway slaves, frequently freed men of social status. Under paralyzing conditions both during and after slavery, a multiplicity of black churches emerged, some on the plantations, others in segregated urban centers, and many along the back roads in rural areas. In each case the black church was the primary community institution owned and controlled by blacks themselves."[30] During the major period of evolution and reconstruction, the black church moved from a mode of survival into a mode of liberation. They sought and found liberation in the form of what E. Franklin Frazier called an agency of social control. These agencies were the development of economic cooperation, education and political life.

Economically, black people began to pool their economic resources to buy buildings and land to develop a sense of independence. Resources were not just for the construction of churches but for the welfare of the people as well, often called mutual societies. They gave support to one another in times of crisis. The black church, with its interior moral norms of preaching, Bible, spirituals and community development, constantly made inroads to the wider public. One of the true reformers of black economic development was the Reverend Washington Browne. In 1876, he succeeded in bringing together in a single organization known as the Grand Foundation of True Reformers, 27 foundations with 2,000 members. This true reformer organized many enterprises such as a weekly newspaper, a bank, real estate, a hotel, and a grocery store. To be sure, many of these ventures were troublesome, however, blacks were learning through cooperation and economical independence, how to exist in the mainstream of things.

The black preacher, oftentimes being the only educated person in most situations, was looked to and called upon to set in place ways of educating others. Many of the educators, after graduation, would be asked by other white missionary instructors to go and build churches and schools, knowing that a way to real independence and liberation was through education. To this day many professional black people owe a large degree of their success to the black church that was grounded in the moral norms of preaching, Bible, spiritual and community development. This created an atmosphere of hospitality, giving nurturing support allowing the person to exist in a world with a sense of dignity and worth.

It became inevitable during the Reconstruction Period that black people would develop a sense of political life. Henry M. Turner, who organized the Negro in the Republican Party in Georgia, was elected to the Georgia Legislature. Bishop James E. Hood of the African Methodist Episcopal Zion Church was elected president of a convention of Negroes in North Carolina. Twenty Negroes were elected to the House of Representatives of the United States from the South during the Reconstruction period. It was the Civil Rights Act of 1867 that allowed blacks to participate in electoral politics. However, the removal of the protection, the unrestrained Ku Klux Klan violence, economic discrimination, and an ever increasing number of restricted black codes and electoral obstacles such as poll taxes and frivolous registration procedures, finally led to a virtually complete disenfranchisement of the black vote in the south. Jim Crow segregation was ratified and legitimized by the highest court in the land, the doctrine of "separate but equal" laid down in the Plessy vs. Ferguson decision of 1896, thus leaving the Black American community without voting rights. While on this Emmaus Road life journey with the wider public, conversations were had but could not be sustained. To offer hospitality to this stranger was then to accept them with

equal regard. As a result, these persons who were disenfran-
chised by the actions of the wider public, returned to the foundational norms of their nurturing which had been the black
church, where their character was reinforced in an atmosphere
of hospitality.

For almost a hundred years from Reconstruction to the Voter
Rights Act of 1965, the black church served as the mainstream
of the black political process. Black people voted and chose
their leaders in their churches. From the pastor to the president
of the women's auxiliaries, this segregated form of politics became the training ground of political experience. With this
kind of in-house training, shaping black people in the exercises
of politics, whenever the obstructive barriers were removed,
the hope was for black people to have an easier transition into
the mainstream of American political life, and life in a broader
context.

At the dawn of the Civil Rights movement there were
many personalities who made significant contributions to
the cause. One such person was the Rev. Adam Clayton
Powell, pastor of the historic Abyssinian Baptist Church in
Harlem. He organized Civil Rights protests against discrimination and economic issues. His base of support in the
protest came from his 8,000-member church. Not only was
Powell a tremendous leader and pastor, but he was also
elected to the United States House of Representatives and
became the chairman of the House Committee on Education
and Labor. His contribution certainly opened doors to the
rise of the Civil Rights Movement.

Another such historical incident that was instrumental in the
acknowledgement of civil rights was the Supreme Court decision of Brown vs. Board of Education in 1954. The decision
showed the injustice of segregated schools and the fallacy of
"separate but equal." It is worth mentioning that Brown was
the Rev. Oliver L. Brown of the St. Mark AME Church in

Topeka, Kansas. Thus, the black church enables one to stand up for the mobilization of the entire race of people.

Using the Emmaus Road narrative, I have, in this section, talked about the journey of the black church as the stranger in its quest to gain entry into the American mainstream. The black church joins the other establishments in history as a stranger, at times walking with them, at other times listening to them, but somehow wanting to be a part of the process of sharing with them. The dark days of loss and resentment could change drastically into a day of joy and celebration if only they could open their eyes and recognize the stranger in their presence. There was no recognition of Jesus on the Emmaus Road until the breaking of bread. After which their eyes were open and the stranger and host traded places. However, in the Civil Rights Movement the reverse took place. There was recognition of Dr. Martin Luther King Jr., who led the Civil Rights Movement. This developed into opportunities to break bread. Their eyes were opened. He presents to the stranger an ecclesiology of hospitality. In considering King's "beloved community" as a hospitality paradigm with the principles of love, justice, forgiveness and reconciliation, one can readily see that the New Testament gospel is the root of this vision. It is the love of God operating in the human spirit that makes genuine relationships; moving people to recognize the other as neighbor and friends. The paradigm of the "beloved community" is not seeking power over them, simply power with them. No person or group of people can ever wholly feel connected to God without the experience and acknowledgement of the other, the stranger in their presence.

King's conception of the "beloved community" is best described as a transformation and regeneration of human society. The "beloved community" would be that of an integrated society. Real relationships are the creation of love and not legislation. King said, "Desegregation will only create a society

where men are physically desegregated but spiritually segregated, where elbows are together and hearts apart."[31] King had
a strong emphasis upon inter-relatedness. Hospitality should
always recognize interconnectedness. King affirms "whatever
affects one directly, affects all indirectly."[32] We are individual
selves but not self-autonomous. We are more than I, we are we.
Cornel West uses the metaphor of jazz, not as a musical art
form, but for a mode of being in the world, to illustrate our interconnectedness and communal interdependence. King interpreted this inter-relatedness to mean that injustice anywhere is
a threat to justice everywhere. King's thought of justice was
not just for black people but for all people.

King's thoughts of the "beloved community" could also be
heard in his I Have A Dream speech delivered during the
March on Washington August 28, 1963. He envisioned a new
social order wherein diverse groups of people would live together as brothers and sisters sharing equally the abundance of
God's creation, knowing there are inherent rights that are God
given, that every human being should enjoy and not privileges
extended by others.

It is agape that creates these relationships. "Love," King says,
"is a community-creating force; it is the only force that can bring
community into existence because its inherent unselfishness
leads to *cooperation* instead of *competition* and *conflict*."[33] The
crucifixion-resurrection and the advent of the Holy Spirit point to
the content of what gives the "beloved community" its hope. The
fellowship called into life by Christ's self-surrender serves to reconcile the world, the suffering of the people and through participation in the working of Christ through the Spirit. The Christian,
being there for others, cannot be detached from being with others in solidarity; and being *with* others cannot be separated from
being *for* others.

Is the actualization of such a community possible? One cannot rush to answer this question. Even King himself acknowl-

edged what he called superficial optimism on one hand and a crippling pessimism on the other as it relates to the elimination of social problems. Change is a slow process. King was fully aware that "beloved community" is a "not yet" but certainly on the way. However, when people of all ethnicities work together, the "not yet" becomes an increasing possibility.

The stranger on the Emmaus Road who joined the two travelers spoke so eloquently about what had transpired until they reached their destination. Then the two travelers gave an invitation to the stranger to join them. He did, and they soon became a community of three. They sat down and broke bread together, and from that sharing, much was discovered. Much is being discovered when we come to the supper table. Eyes are still being opened, hearts are still set on fire, and we realize that we are all one mutually united together. Therefore, the church that reflects hospitality as an ecclesiological practice of ministry and a public way of life must reflect and represent the lordship of Jesus Christ. This means the church cannot adapt its social order— from the way the society in which it lives— is run, or allow its Christian practice to be determined by a worldly agenda, for it has to correspond to its Lord and then represent new life for society. It cannot be a racial church, which permits racial separation and discrimination within its own fellowship. It cannot be a class church. It cannot be a male church. It must be neither Jew nor Greek; neither slave nor free, neither male nor female, but *one in Christ*. This oneness is found in the fellowship of the Lord's Supper offering many possibilities such as seeing the interconnectedness of the world in all people.

The concluding chapter will look at hospitality as a covenant paradigm that addresses the issues of liberation and justice as ways to encourage unity that honors the practice of hospitality.

Chapter IV

HOSPITALITY AS COVENANT MAKING

While hospitality has been an important perspective that enables one to see the other who was once a stranger, hospitality is also the means by which persons can enter into a covenant relationship. I will, in this chapter, look at hospitality as a paradigm for covenant, laying out an ethical framework of justice, lifting the biblical notions of covenant, and addressing the issues of liberation as ways to encourage the practice of hospitality.

One way that this can happen is to consider hospitality as a covenant paradigm. The Bible, which houses stories of oppression and other forms of injustices, tells how God acted on behalf of the oppressed creating opportunities for covenant along the way, and then becomes the voice for all who are oppressed.

The covenantal notion that gives credence to the subject of hospitality is the covenant God has with God's people. Much of how I come to understand covenant is from the Judeo-Christian perspective that undergirds the practice of hospitality. The biblical models of hospitality are also painted with the brush of covenant. The initial story of Abram's calling serves as the catalyst that connects hospitality and covenant.

God initiates a call to Abram in covenantal form that is laden with well-being and hospitality. What follows are some amazing stories of hospitality that serve to protect the covenant that God made with Abram (Genesis 20-23). Pivotal in this covenant paradigm is the exodus event (Exodus 1-15). The author of Exodus recites the story in great detail. The Hebrew people suffered and cried out for help. God heard and enlisted Moses to take leadership as a negotiator for the sake of Hebrew freedom. Pharaoh would not hear. God intervened in miraculous ways to liberate the Hebrews from Egyptian bondage, (remembering the covenant that extended beyond Abraham to include Israel). The exodus story became Israel's creed and was stated in capsulated form: "We were Pharaoh's slaves in Egypt, but the Lord brought us out of Egypt with a mighty hand (Deuteronomy 6:21). The continuation of this covenant paradigm is found in the person of Jesus Christ, who in the tradition of the exodus, championed the cause of liberation. For Jesus, liberation was more than a concept, it was action empowered by God. He says, quoting Isaiah 61:

> *The spirit of the Lord is upon me because he has anointed me to bring good news to the poor. He has sent me to proclaim release to the captives, and recovery of sight to the blind, to let the oppressed go free, to proclaim the year of the Lord's favor. Today this scripture is fulfilled in your hearing.*
>
> Luke 4:18–19, 21

Jesus, in His ministry as proclaimed in His inaugural, reached out in solidarity to others demonstrating that the God He preached about and prayed to was a God of covenant and liberation. People who were enslaved and oppressed were being set free by Jesus in the name of this God of the exodus and covenant. People, who were sick, poor, demon-possessed and persecuted found in Jesus a form of liberation covenant. Jesus said, "It is not those who are healthy who need a physician, but those who are sick; I did not come to call the righteous, but sinners" (Mark 2:17). Jesus sought out people in society who seemed to lack something. His ministry impacted those most in need of liberation.

Jesus crosses boundaries, placed by society, to get to some. There is one story after another that depicts Jesus doing something with someone who was considered a social outcast. The following narrative snapshots below are just brief examples of the daily work and ministry of Jesus as He interacts with the powerless for the sake of liberation, hospitality and covenant.

There was a naked man called Legion who lived in the graveyard. Everyone was afraid of him. Jesus clothed him in his right mind and sent him home.

Mark 5:1–20 Paraphrased

He met a woman at the well whom he asked to give him a drink of water. The woman said to Him, "How is it that you, a Jew, ask me, a Samaritan woman, for a drink?" Jesus offers her living water. She leaves her water pots running into the city saying, "Come see a man who told me of all the things that I have done." Is this the Christ?

John 4:4–43 Paraphrased

There was a woman who was caught in adultery, and the religious leaders were ready to stone her to death. Jesus gave a lecture on hypocrisy, and they all dropped their stones and left. Then he told the woman to go and Honor God.

John 8:3–11 Paraphrased

These are just a few of the many liberating events that Jesus caused to happen in the lives of people who were oppressed in some way. However, the death of Jesus, in the struggle for liberation, became God's defining covenantal moment. God performed the ultimate act of liberation by raising Jesus from the

dead. The resurrection symbolizes God's victory over the enemies of life. It is to this extent that the resurrection validates
Jesus' message and serves as a symbol of the triumph of justice for the human community. This community of the oppressed is shaped by Exodus-Resurrection, hospitality and
covenant, for the sake of liberation.

As I move from the biblical notion of Exodus-Resurrection
which shaped hospitality and covenant for the sake of liberation, the church, to a larger degree, now becomes the covenant
community offering hospitality as a means for all to experience
God's grace in the world. The covenant paradigm and the
shaping of hospitality ecclesiologically depends upon the
shared experience of remembering the biblical narratives. Biblical remembrance, coupled with historical experience develops an alternative for combating injustice in the world. However, when the church forgets the truth of its identity, an
identity that is shaped by the stories of exodus-resurrection,
memory is lost leading to silent partnering with the injustices
in the world. When the contemporary church becomes so en-
culturated to the American ethos, it loses its power to transform the culture, because it has lost its capacity to remember.
As Karen Lebacqz says, "In short, justice is grounded in remembrance."[34] It is hard to imagine the church taking a stance
against cultural injustices without the sensitivity of remembrance that is necessary for such a position.

The purpose of the church is to reveal an alternative way of
perceiving and living life in the world. The thoughts of some
that social transformation should be left to God's unraveling is
a contradiction of Christian gospel. It is important that the
church accept the responsibility of integrating Christ's vision
into the pragmatic realities of the world. The church must remember the liberating process, that the God Who became incarnate and acts in this world takes seriously its social structures. For example, if the church remains silent on the issues of

racism and sexism because it is concerned about the tarnishing of its good standing in the eyes of the wider community, then the church is not being the alternative covenant community. There is a sensitivity that is necessary, born out of an alternative consciousness that would render any form of oppression practices of sin.

One main reason for silence has been that slavery and sexism were both justified in the Christian tradition. The story of the nation of Ham, who was cursed by his father, Noah, has been cited historically to support discrimination against black people. Karen Lebacqz says, "Christianity has been an instrument for the reign of injustice. What should have been a tool for the spread of love, peace and freedom in the world has been at times a tool for spreading terror, injustice and repression."[35] It appears that because of this, black people historically have been used as a human experiment, always trying out for new rules or theories simply to be counted as human. The institution of slavery was supported by good bible-carrying oppressors. Therefore, if the dehumanization of a race of people is to be seen as unjust, there must emerge a hermeneutic that includes those who are oppressed. It is the church that develops this hermeneutic of hospitality and covenant that is against any form of injustice. The world of the oppressed and the oppressor is not the same world. Lebacqz uses the analogy of the birds of the air and the fish of the sea to make clear the point of different human realities. She says, "Oppressors and the oppressed do not inhabit the same world. The struggles of the oppressed against their ocean of unjust forces are very different for the oppressor to understand."[36] What is then needed is for oppressed people to find their voice and speak for themselves.

Such is also the case with sexism in the Bible. Just as Christianity justified slavery, the Bible has been used to illustrate women as weak, crafty and evil. There is the story of Adam and Eve where Eve becomes the perpetrator of the garden event leading Adam astray (Ge 2).

Then there is the sexual abuse of Tamar by her brother, Amnon. After Amnon rapes Tamar, he sends her away in disgrace. As in many infamous, contemporary cases, the blame is shifted to the female victim. "She should not have been in his bedroom" was a popular justification. It would appear that one would expect serious condemnation from David as well as the entire family for this grievous act committed against this woman, but it did not happen. Absalom, who is the brother of Tamar and Amnon, revenges the injustice committed against his sister by killing his brother. David, the father, grieves the death of Amnon but not for Tamar's disgrace as it relates to her being raped (2 Samuel 13:30). Also, the contemporary argument that is posed in male-dominated Christian institutions is that Jesus is God incarnate, Jesus is male. Jesus called twelve male disciples. Therefore, God must be represented by males. Many churches continued to adopt this unjust theological twisting of biblical text, thus treating women as third-class citizens.

There is no argument for the injustices of oppression and sexism; they still remain ungodly acts of violence. Bringing this violence under subjection includes finding ways for the perpetrators to see themselves in this violent act. One such starting point is the injustices themselves. Lebacqz says, "If justice begins with the correction of injustice, then the most important tools for understanding justice will be the stories of injustice as experienced by the oppressed and the tool of social and historical analysis that help to illumine the process by which those historical injustices arose and the meaning of them in the lives of the victims."[37] Televised coverage of clashes during the Civil Rights Movement generated a growing sensitivity in the wider public to what was happening to black folk. For the first time, whites saw other whites unleash dogs, turn on high-powered water hoses on those who marched for their rights and blatant police brutality captured on film. When seeing this kind of blatant disregard for human life, either through embarrassment, shame or a real connection with the humanity of the *other*, social change was under way. There was a move in the direction of justice because injustice captured an audience. Justice is a story. The story of justice is told from the story of injustice.

In telling the story of justice, the story of injustice finds a stage. Such a stage is the church where hospitality and covenant are practiced. The ethical decision that needs to be made in light of this is to determine whose story is told. Injustice is a creature that has many dimensions. One could say that injustice has its own covenant. Once a person is dehumanized, then every other category of that person's existence simply follows suit. There is no hope economically, politically, socially or educationally because the person who is oppressed is not valued in the eyes of the oppressor. If there is to be political or economical justice, the story of the oppressed must emerge as the story that carries all the stories of hurting humanity. For the many who are oppressed, deciding ethically whose story gets told also determines if any story is heard.

In a kind of paradoxical way there are times when we are challenged to tell what something is by saying what it is not. The same holds true with respect to naming the root of justice. One can better tell the story of what justice *is* from the perspective of injustice.

Justice will participate in the biblical narrative. God of Exodus and Resurrection is also Lord of the church whose purpose is best served in creating covenant. Justice will reside in responsibility and duty, not in rights. There is with justice mutual care, one for the other. The primary injustice is oppression. This breech of covenant really affects both the oppressed and oppressor. And, with the oppressed, there is a disconnection between them and their oppressor. With the oppressor there is a disconnection between them and God. Hospitality seeks covenant, not simply with God, but with humanity as well.

I have mentioned that when the church loses its power to transform, it has also lost its power to speak. However, when the oppressed find their voice to speak, the oppressors lose their power to control. The oppressed strangely enough found their voice in and with the same book that was used to oppress them—the Bible.

Therefore, the Bible which houses stories of oppression and other forms of injustice, tells how God acted on behalf of the oppressed creating opportunities for covenant along the way, and then becomes the voice for all who are oppressed. It is a theology from the other side, where biblical remembrance is coupled with historical experience, and alternatives develop for combating injustice. This method depends upon the oppressed knowing the biblical narrative, seeing how the narrative speaks to their historical experiences, and finding a way for this story to be told. In telling the story, new hopes emerge and old fears dissipate. The story that is told is that God is on the side of the oppressed for the sake of human community. It is not a story that necessarily isolates, that is not the intent in telling it. However, when told from the perspective of the oppressed, and heard by the oppressor, there is the possibility of repentance, and with repentance, the hope of hospitality and covenant. This is the aim of hospitality as a covenant paradigm; that is, by hearing the story of others, creating the living possibility of what the Bible calls the Kingdom of God.

Although I am speaking from a Christian perspective, hospitality as a covenant paradigm is not an exclusive paradigm. Covenantal hospitality does not seek uniformity, but instead, calls for unity. It is a way for the people of the world to share differences as a learning experience and to share a basic oneness, our humanity.

Enoch Oglesby uses the concept of "covenant-harambee" to get at this idea. This is a unity that celebrates diversity. One can easily forget the covenantal mandate of Christ and begin to work toward human structures that are suspicious, divisive and hostile. "Covenant-Harambee," says Oglesby, "is descriptive of the suffering love of Jesus going to bat for the groaning of all creation together, so that none may be lost and all may experience the triumphant power of God's Kingdom of righteousness and reconciling grace throughout the land."[38] Harambee is an African expression of unity which carries with it similarities to the Hebraic expression of covenant. Combining these two terms, we are given insight into the importance of developing a critical consciousness as it relates to racism and other social evils that deepen the divide of the human condition.

Harambee is not simply tied to the notion of unity, but kinship and community as well. For example, in African society the moral agent is an individual whose personal identity possesses virtue and standing only in relation to the social reality of the community. So then, as one member of the family or kinship suffers, all suffer: when one rejoices the whole village rejoices. To take seriously this notion of covenant. Harambee is to live toward a vision of shalom. The Hebraic expression of covenant and the Swahili expression of community, when merged together give an alternative to the dominant Eurocentric notion of ethical discourse that has done little in addressing the problem of race in America. One does not have to be reminded that race in America is a nasty, messy situation. However, one does have to be reminded that the mess victimizes all of us as all of humanity is interconnected, interdependent, and communal. To embrace Covenant-Harambee is to understand this human interconnectedness and to begin to see others and ourselves as part of a greater whole.

To take hospitality as a covenant paradigm further is to see the world as one with many nations, and all nations having realized their interdependence with the others. The United Nations symbolizes this hope. We have a kind of world community that is before us, and the possibility of isolation of any kind would be fatal. What Oglesby said about Covenant-Harambee as a principle for unity is meaningful here, "Either we hang together in the struggle against racism, sexism and European imperialism or we just hang."[39] Either we find a way to live and work together in world community, or we perish. When seen from this angle, hospitality as a covenant paradigm, does not seek to convert the other to one's point of view, but hopes to establish an ongoing conversation where all parties could see it as both a divine gift and positive human activity. I agree with what Birch and Rasmussen say about this process. They say, "Whether we look at the formation of a people of God in the Exodus, Sinai drama, or at the Cross, Pentecost account, the experience of divine power as a power for people-hood."[40] In essence, this is an experience of God as the One who generates community as the deepest of meaning. Our commonality in covenant and expression of hospitality that flows from the community's life together is centered in the divine power of God.

In Matthew 28:19–20, the disciples are given a mandate to go into the world and make disciples. It appears in Acts 2 on the day of Pentecost when the disciples were empowered by the Holy Spirit, that the world the disciples were being sent to, has for a moment, come to them.

Amazingly, in Acts 2 not only were the disciples empowered by the Holy Spirit as God's sign of God's continuing presence with them, but also they began to speak a new language, and, in speaking, were heard by persons who were present from every nation under heaven. Parthians, Medes, Elamites residents of Mesopotamia, Judea, Cappadocia, Egypt, Libya, Pamphylia, Cyrene—all heard them speak of the mighty deeds of God. In speaking, the disciples are heard by the people and in hearing, all the people of the world were amazed that they heard them speaking; each one of them the other's language.

This language is not a mere projection of human ideals and wishes being published by disillusioned followers of Jesus, but instead, a move of God that gathers persons of all kinds to hear the truth of the gospel that belongs to all humanity. To embrace hospitality as a covenant paradigm is to be willing to embrace all the peoples of the world. Although the church is a community that practices hospitality and covenant making, the gift of hospitality and the opportunity for covenant making is given to the world.

Additionally, with the world becoming less Western, less Christian, perhaps even less religious, it becomes increasingly more important for the Christian church to understand its identity and mission. The more deeply we trust what we believe the more hospitable we become in hearing the other voices of the world. Hospitality as covenant-making not only provides a means of acknowledging religious pluralism, but will enable Christians to have a deeper realization of their own covenant faith. The basis of Christian unity is found in Jesus Christ. Peter C. Hodgeson says, "Creeds and theologies are attempts at understanding what the confession of faith in Christ means under different historical circumstances and in relation to specific issues."[41] However, unity cannot be based on creeds or on doctrinal purity, or biblical literalism, but on diversity, plurality and difference. In this respect, unity is much like love, for love demands the recognition of difference and its preservation even as it is taken up into unity. Love means entering into a self-transforming relationship with that which is genuinely and radically other. Without the diverse perspective of God's rainbow of humanity we cannot grasp the truth of the biblical stories. It is the aim of hospitality as a covenant paradigm to accept the fundamental oneness of the human family. Hearing the story of the "other" establishes realities that otherwise would not exist, and then move in the direction of establishing covenant.

I have, for the most part, been expressing ecclesiologically how this paradigm of hospitality as covenant might work in the broad arena of the world. Now I want to share what this paradigm looks like in the practice of ministry at the Shalom Church.

The basic principles that guide hospitality as covenant-making in the practice of ministry at the Shalom Church is "remembrance." Those who practice ministry must be asked to remember. Remember not simply the journey of Shalom Church but also the many times in life when displacement made one feel like a stranger. Thus, being the stranger is fundamental to the human experience. In times of abundance and complacency we all have to be reminded to remember. This is true of Israel in the commandment they were given by Moses:

All the commandments that I am commanding you today you shall be careful to do, that you may live and multiply and go in and possess the land which the Lord swore to give you. You shall remember all the ways which the Lord your God has led you in the wilderness these forty years. That He might humble you, testing you to know what was in your heart, whether you keep His commandment or not.

Deuteronomy 8:1–2

This was also true of Jesus who gives the disciples a sacramental identity and establishes covenant by sharing with them one sacramental need. The meal, when served, calls for the sacramental life of Jesus.

For I received from the Lord that which I also delivered to you, that the Lord Jesus in the night in which he was betrayed took bread; And when He had given thanks, He broke it and said, "This is My body which is for you; do this in remembrance of

*Me", In the same way He took the cup also after saying, "This
cup is the new covenant in My blood—do this as often as you
drink it, in remembrance of me.*

I Corinthians 11:23–25

Since remembering was fundamental for Israel as a
covenant people as well as for Jesus in His ministry as He fulfilled covenant, the same should be true for Shalom Church.
When confronted by the stranger, and there is within the host
a sensitivity for their well-being, hospitality should be extended without expecting anything in return. For hospitality as
covenant-making is best witnessed in response to basic human
needs—needs that arise from poverty, marital conflict, stress,
domestic violence, unemployment, substance-abuse and various social ills.

The Shalom Church, in the practice of hospitality as
covenant-making, seeks to affirm people. Black people need
affirmation. It is important in the practice of ministry at the
Shalom Church to see hospitality as a way that meets human
needs. Occasionally when reminded of terrible acts of violence, which create doubts, fears and hostilities, the affirmation of one's person-hood is required. Without affirming one's
blackness there could develop an identity crisis. As a way of
affirming blackness, James Cone offers black theology as "survival theology." In black survival theology he explains three
characteristics of the black condition: tension between life and
death, identity crisis and white social and political power. With
respect to the social and political power Cone says,

"To be human is a condition of social oppression and involves
affirming that which the oppressor regards as degrading. In a
world in which the oppressor defines rights in terms of white-
ness, humanity means unqualified identification with blackness. Black, therefore is beautiful; oppressors have made it

ugly. We glorify it because they despise it, we love it because
they hate it."[42]

Hospitality as covenant would suggest it does not matter
who likes your blackness or hates blackness, you are who you
are because God made you. God is the principal player in your
creation. It also affirms hospitality as covenant affirms the cultural expression of blackness.

There is also the thought of self-liberation meaning there
are persons in the worship experience who need to be set
free on a personal level. They are, in the worship, experiencing psychological and spiritual bondage. Hospitality as
covenant socially is not enough. Hospitality as covenant-
making attempts to liberate such persons through the gospel
of Jesus Christ. For instance, in the worship at Shalom
Church, we have what is traditionally known as "altar call."
The altar call in the black church as part of the worship
liturgy is the time when worshippers unite themselves at the
altar and the pastor prays for all persons simultaneously.
However, at Shalom, instead of gathering collectively at the
altar for prayer, persons are asked to organize themselves in
small groups. For every group, a prayer leader is assigned.
There are three things of significance that happen: there is a
greeting and name sharing, each person gives voice to a particular concern, and together we enter into prayer covenants.
This is the most intimate part of worship, and the place
where hospitality as a covenant paradigm can be experienced. With greeting and sharing of names, we are saying
persons are forbidden to remain strangers in worship. Elizabeth Geitz says, "When we make a decision to welcome all
strangers, we become a link in the chain of hospitality that
reached back through Sarah and Abraham, through Jesus
and Armanias, through countless Christians throughout the
centuries."[43]

Moreover, we become a part of that growing community which honors hospitality. We are no longer surprised to see that strangers we've met in the community are now a part of the prayer gathering. When we become greeters in the art of worship, a kind of "ecclesiogenesis" is being formulated into a sacred relationship where God is present. As we welcome the stranger, we become bestowers of guest-friendship reflecting our past journey as Shalom Church and also reflecting the biblical expectation. There is both a giving and receiving that reflects the importance of covenant to receive the Word of God. Jesus said, "Where two or three are gathered in my name, I am there among them" (Matthew 18:20). Additionally, to ask the stranger his name is moving to a level where something may be revealed that goes beyond mere naming. We are always greater than our name indicates; our name is the starting point of an unfolding history.

There are those who enter the various prayer circles who feel that they have lost their place in the world. They have experienced all kinds of abuse and have even abused themselves but somehow find sanity at this moment. However, this time of worship and prayer is not a quick cure or instant therapy, but a life long work that finds its meaning in hospitality as covenant-making.

Each person has an opportunity to offer up prayer requests in the presence of others. The facilitator would again lead the way in this process. A certain amount of vulnerability is required in this sharing. Not only is the conversation in the context of the prayer circle important, but the formation as well. They give opportunity to enhance community which leads to covenant. As each person gives voice to a particular concern, it is the responsibility of the facilitator to both speak and listen. Speaking and listening are permanent in a ministry of hospitality. Those who are facilitating listen with the intent to recall. It is the request of the stranger in the circle that deserves the utmost attention. There are moments of vulnerability during the sharing of one's concerns that are always present when hospitality as covenant-making is being extended. However, it is the sharing of names and the openness of greeting each other in this step of the process that makes speaking and listening possible.

In reference to speaking, the facilitator is asked not just to speak but to pay attention to the various ways in which speaking takes place. For example, verbal communication is not the only means of communicating. People speak just as profoundly with facial expressions as well as body dynamics. It is always helpful in knowing what to do when the facilitators of the formation of hospitality as covenant-making are aware of these dimensions. In Henri Nouwen's *Reaching Out: Three Movements of the Spiritual Life* he says, "Someone who is filled with ideas, concepts, opinions, and convictions cannot be a good host. There is no inner space to listen, no openness to discover the gift of the other. A good host not only has to be poor in mind but also in heart. When our hearts are filled with prejudice, worries, jealousies, etc., there is little room for the stranger."[44] It is the sharing of names and the respect for space at the moment of greeting the other that takes place. This brings a level of understanding and community for the process of speaking and listening.

After concerns have been addressed, the facilitator gives back to the others what they have heard from serious listening. It is these concerns that are prayed about in the intimacy of the circle. What is interesting is that there are anywhere between 15 to 20 groups assembled all over the building preparing to pray at the same time. One would think this presents a challenge that is not necessary in organizing people for prayer. This is certainly challenging, however, it is worth all that we can give of ourselves to see people make a spiritual connection with God, themselves, and the community where they are being nurtured. This could be considered an alternative prayer liturgy creating hospitality and covenant.

These groups assembled over the building provide a visual for understanding the many sub-groups that exist in the culture and even in the world. It is not uniformity that hospitality seeks, but unity. These groups speak to the awesome power of God who is able to acknowledge the *many* and the *one*. This time of group prayer is a way the Shalom Church shows hospitality to the stranger, and becomes the recipient of the stranger's gift. In all, hospitality is becoming an ecclesiological practice of ministry and a way that shapes covenant in community. There are some other tenets of hospitality, as covenant-making that remain a work in progress that will enhance the practice of ministry at the Shalom Church. Let us now turn in our discussion to some critical observations in regard to a summary of the essential theme of our theological inquiry.

Chapter V

Summary: Hospitality Findings and Proclamation

I was interested in hospitality, initially, as a word that was used continually and passionately by people who visited Shalom Church (City of Peace). They would say to others and me, "This church has the gift of *hospitality*." I did not have a clue as to the many meanings this word had. What *hospitality* meant to me was . . . whatever they said about our church at least we impacted them in one way; they said we were "nice."

Two things happened as I engaged myself in conversation with this issue of *hospitality*. First, I discovered that hospitality is too much of a responsibility for only the Shalom Church (City of Peace), and for that matter any other church, to shoulder. Hospitality, as a gift, can be shared, experienced and embraced, but never controlled. Moreover, if the gift was operating in our presence and we were unaware, how much more effective in ministry could we become if we took seriously the notion of hospitality and intended it as a Christian practice? Also, how could we move in the direction to make this gift not something that we did, but a response to who we are in Jesus Christ. The practical work of any congregation will not last long on compliments or pure emotions. That which is experienced and celebrated in the church must be grounded in the

gospel of Jesus Christ. Hospitality, to be a gift of the Shalom
Church, must become an ecclesiological practice of ministry.
Those disciples who make up the congregation must see hospitality as something shared by the *many* instead of the *few*.
The concept of ministry being departmentalized, dividing the
church into little categories, must give way to the new paradigm of hospitality. Hospitality, working as an ecclesiological
practice of the church, will have far-reaching implications.
When the practice is intentional, it will become embedded in
one's lifestyle. Every encounter with the "other" will be
viewed through the lens of hospitality. Just as other gifts have
to be nurtured and developed for maximum use, the same
holds true for hospitality. Hospitality must be practiced if
we are to arrive at a deeper understanding of what it means to
live as Christians in changing times such as these. We want to
know what our faith has to do with improving our careers, developing friendships, raising our children and strengthening
our marriages. When hospitality is nurtured and becomes an
ecclesiological practice, these answers will emerge along with
those to many other questions.

Before I started to take these issues seriously, I thought,
that *the* church, *my* church, *your* church, and *any* church that
had its historical orientations grounded in the narrative we
call the Bible, also operates on the truth about how this world
is to be run and how the gifts are to be dispersed. It was only
after starting this work that I moved in the direction of repentance. To see the church from such a narrow perspective
is to offer the world *hostility* instead of *hospitality*. It is to
deny the fact that not only is the church in the world, but the
world is in the church. The church is not all good and the
world is not totally evil. The church is not always faithful nor
is the world consistently unfaithful. The church is not always
wise nor is the world always foolish. The church does not always know God's will or live in harmony with God while the

world is ignorant or estranged from God's will. The church's mission is simply to live faithful, practice hospitality, and leave the results with God. Hospitality is a gift given to the world in which the church is included. I think that there is this sense of security in the human narrative where some, out of their security, would define themselves as host. The church may be guilty of this. The host seems to always have the upper hand. However, while the host entertains the stranger, it is the host that leaves the encounter with a different perspective simply because the stranger, "the other," has gifts to share that were never anticipated.

For the last five years, the Berkeley neighborhood has hosted the Shalom Church. This was not understood initially. What was understood was that we were more prepared to host than was the surrounding community. We were the Church! We have all the resources, gifts, and religious experiences. The Berkeley neighborhood was the typical urban setting surrounded by poverty and crime with nothing to offer. However, upon reflection, a better understanding of how hospitality operates as a gift in and outside the church emerged. The Berkeley neighborhood was also the host. It was their narrative of which we became a part and hoped to eventually share ours with them. The dialectic of receiver/giver, host/stranger was never truer. Fundamentally, humanity always moves from host/stranger to stranger/host. In Christian theology, the giver and receiver are worthy of equal regard. Since there are no permanent positions in life with persons always moving in and out of situations where they sometimes experience being the host and other times the stranger, hospitality becomes the means by which equal regard and moral obligation are exercised.

In keeping with the idea of hospitality being the world's gift in which the church is included, and the living out of this gift with all parties being interconnected, there is another development that is critical for our understanding, that is the "self" as a stranger.

As God creates us anew, challenging us, calling us, leading us, we may at times feel like a stranger to ourselves. We may marvel at the person we are becoming, yet dread the road God uses to get us there. It is here where reaching out to another, just as a stranger would seek the host and a mutual sharing of the experience, can not only be reassuring but a means to develop community as well.

The second thing that happened as I engaged in conversation with the issue of hospitality, was that I began to see proclamation from a different perspective.

Clergy and laity would agree that preaching is a vital part of Christian ministry. It is also probably fair to estimate that excellence in preaching is an essential ingredient in the life of a healthy congregation. However, preaching does not happen because the preacher stands up and begins to expound in sermonic form. There is a great deal of preparation that goes into the preaching moment: the potential to shape persons in one way or another in the practice of ministry. Now, because there are various preaching methods, and a variety of ways to prepare, keeping in mind some have had the benefits of an excellent college and seminary experience that covered biblical studies as well as a comprehensive look at other disciplines that broaden ones' area of knowledge. While on the other hand there are those who have had a very narrow training experience that limits their ability to interpret scripture holistically.

Regardless of the category in which the preacher finds himself or herself, I think that a pursuit of some preparation holds true for all preachers. With respect to hospitality and preaching, there is a connection and preparation. The text that is being analyzed is, in this instance, considered the stranger. The preacher looking at the text becomes the host waiting patiently for the text to unfold, hoping that the unfolding might be shared in the proclamation. William E. Dorman and Ronald J. Allen talk about the text as a stranger. They say,

"A text is another who claims our attention and who makes its own witness concerning God and the world. Sometimes a periscope seems to talk with the preacher in sweet tones of a new lover, sometimes in the stern voice of an angry judge, sometimes in melancholy, sometimes in extravagance that has gone beyond itself. The voices of the Bible are as many as the grains of sand on the seashore."[45]

Preparation for preaching is necessary because the text somehow always appears as a stranger, willing to speak. If a relationship is going to develop between preacher and text, an investigation that allows the text to speak must take place.

In the language of hospitality-host/stranger commonality— what am I to do with a text as part of my anticipated interaction and investigation is called "exegesis." To exegete is to consider the social/historical critical method of treating and locating the text for answers. This process is necessary because the preacher/host comes to the occasion with her/his own predisposition. There are prejudices, biases and intuitions that may prevent them from hearing the text, thusly, creating a monologue of their own reflections. Delia Halverson says, "Hospitality is showing how much you care for another person before expounding on how much you know."[46] The same holds true for the treatment of a text. Although a text may appear to be an inanimate object, these are real people from the past who look to have conversation with the preacher of the present age. The text brings real gifts and a point of view that would not have been realized without an opportunity for conversation. Thomas G. Lane says in *The Senses of Preaching*, that "before a preacher *says* something, a preacher must *see* something. To be a preacher is to be a witness, one who sees before speaking, one whose right to speak is created by what has been seen."[47]

Preparing to preach is not for communal compliments but to be a witness in the world for Jesus Christ, shaping people to share that witness in a practice of hospitality. Also, in keeping with the idea of preparation as a way for hospitality and proclamation to interact, one must realize that not only are the eyes for hospitality and preaching discovered in study, but a voice emerges as well from the same discipline. This is not saying something loudly, however, having something to say with volume. Volume is never a substitute for content. Therefore, the voice that is heard in proclamation is the voice that is found in preparation. Thomas Lane says, "Finding something to say does not come from a set of techniques or getting hold of the right sermon-help resources, but rather from an ongoing process of reflection and study which produces mixed yields. Biblical texts have claims to make upon us, things they wish to say, texts that once were preached, and wish to be preached again."[48]

As I continue to investigate the beauty of hospitality and proclamation interacting as does the host and stranger, there is another element that surfaces in the preacher's preparations that needs to be addressed. Unnoticed is the fact that not all texts are friendly, hospitable, community-unifying texts. These are texts that are abrasive, hostile, and could be considered oppressive. For instance, Paul states in Ephesians 6:5

Slaves, be obedient to those who are your masters, according to the flesh, with fear and trembling, in the sincerity of your heart, as to Christ.

Remember, not only does the text speak to the preacher from a historical context, the preacher speaks also to the text from a cultural context. All of this is important in determining what kind of preaching shapes hospitality. The preacher who emerges from study having played host to texts that are sometimes friendly, sometimes hostile, sometimes an acquaintance, and sometimes an evolving relationship, must make a moral and spiritual decision on what to use and what not to use for the sake of a healthy congregation. But, he realizes that the aim of preaching is to witness to the truth of God found in Jesus Christ, and the creating of community that honors hospitality.

Just as a union of hospitality develops between the preacher and text through the process of study, we now seek a union between preacher and hearers of the message for a shaping of community that practices hospitality. I raised the question earlier about the impact hospitality had on proclamation or whether proclamation impacted hospitality. The answer is simple; these two gifts simultaneously work together. Hospitality creates the space necessary for preaching to be heard, and preaching shapes the hearer so hospitality can be practiced. Moreover, just as hospitality and proclamation are simultaneously working together, so must the preacher in his/her preaching work to unify the message and the hearers. The miracle of community happens within the rich context of sharing, when both preacher and hearers match an eagerness, openness and regard the need for oneness. The preacher is sent forth to proclaim a message of God and human togetherness. When this message is heard, the possibilities of genuine hospitable community are limitless. Through the message, the hearers must sense that a practice of hospitality depends on the vitality of other practices. Hospitality is bound up with issues of forgiveness and the ordering of communities. This leads us to consider questions about boundaries and barriers; or Sabbath rest, which is necessary for reshaping our commitment of *offering* and *receiving* hospitality, or singing a communal activity that can be a life-fransforming experience. These are some of the experiences that Dorothy Bass lists in *Practicing Our Faith* that when seen as being cultivated together becomes an ecclesiological practice of the church. However, when each practice seeks its own way to do its own thing, its results will be that of division and disunity. The sermon therefore must be "engagingly" clear, and the preacher must be expressively focused in creating a listening community that will practice hospitality. The central message of the preacher for the shaping process should be one of togetherness. Preaching is a divine assignment given for the sake of propelling human togetherness lived in the celebration of God. This message (in the context of the local Christian assembly) is inclusive of all. Moreover, the idea of the message and the hearers of the message being united, shaping hospitality as an ecclesiological practice has implication beyond the local fellowship. The gifts of hospitality and proclamation, when released, cannot be contained by any institution. There is a broader context where hospitality must be practiced, and the gospel proclaimed in the context of the world.

Parker Palmer, in his book *The Company of Strangers* contends that Christian community forms in reaction to life in the larger society. He says, "When people look upon the church, it is not of importance that they be instructed by our theology or *altered by our ethic* but that they may be moved by the quality of our life together."[49] The church, given these gifts of hospitality and proclamation, is not to practice these gifts in isolation, away from the public world, but they are to be shared for the transforming of the culture. What has been proclaimed and what has been heard, forming a union, must now be lived out in community. Jesus said in commissioning the disciples in Matthew 28:19-20:

> *Go therefore and make disciples of all nations, baptizing in the name of the Father and Son and the Holy Spirit teaching them to observe all that I have commanded you; and lo, I am with you always, even to the end of the age.*

While contemplating to what extent the preacher is to extend him/herself in the practice of hospitality and proclamation, I turn to Jesus Christ, who is the embodiment of both proclamation (word) and hospitality (deed) in the flesh. Jesus is the living expression of God's love for humanity. Colossians 1:17 says,

He is before all things, and in Him all things hold together.

Word and deed, creation and creature, hospitality and proclamation are held together by Jesus. The gospel of John makes this point clear. John 1:14 says,

And the word became flesh, and dwelt among us and we saw his glory.

In the Johannine writings, the meaning of the word takes on new dimension. In John, the word is not gospel, but instead, person, the person of Jesus. All that the prophetic word was *before* Him is *now* Him. For proclamation this is not a message to deliver, but a person to know.

Finally, preaching is paramount at the Shalom Church. However, it is not the preaching that makes the worship, it is the worship that makes the preaching. Worship is central because everything that Christians do is grounded in the essential activity of worship. All other activities flow from the concentration of worship. Included in that is preaching. If hospitality is to be an ecclesiological practice of the Shalom Church, it must be shaped by preaching. I hope that in the days to come and conversation between hospitality and preaching continues, that perhaps a new hermeneutic of hospitality will emerge. I believe that Shalom Church exists *in* God and *for* God with sensitivity for others. We carry with us the remembrance of our journey, and to a greater degree, the remembrance of God's word and deeds, both the death and the resurrection. Truly, if we have any gifts at all, it is because God has given graciously to us to dispense as an act of grace. I will share with you a sermon (found in the Appendix) that I have preached at the Shalom Church which I hope gives integrity to the notion of hospitality and discloses the possibilities of these two practices calling forth God's church.

APPENDIX: Who is My Neighbor? Luke 10:25–37

(Preached at Shalom Church—August 1999)

It starts as the lawyer's question seeking to justify himself and turns out to be our question searching for boundaries in a world full of people who are unlike us. Who is my neighbor provokes debate and uneasiness in the world. The Pharisees, rabbis, common people—all drawing the line at different places. Today the question is even more complex. Modern mobility makes countless numbers of people across the world, in a few fleeting moments, our neighbor. We stand beside them in elevators, walk past them in malls, sit next to them on airplanes and rejoice or agonize with them at sporting events. There seems to be no endless claim to this question, no boundary. "Who is my neighbor?"

I have discovered that the motive in which we ask the question is just as important as the answer. For instance, the lawyer wanted to justify himself by narrowing this concept to include the few and not the many. The question the lawyer poses seeks to limit responsibility rather than defend responsibilities. He was perhaps more interested in theological speculation than in practical application.

In responding to the lawyer's question, Jesus tells a parable about the neighbor. A parable is a physical truth that portrays a spiritual reality. In this parable Jesus opens the possibility of where and how we meet our neighbor. Jesus says,

> *A man was going down from Jerusalem to Jericho, and fell among robbers and they stripped him and beat him, and went away leaving him half-dead. And by chance a priest was going down the road and saw him, but instead of helping him, passed by on the other side. Likewise did the Levite. But a Samaritan, who was on a journey, came up to him and when he saw him felt compassion. He treated the wounds of the man, put him on his beast and brought him to an inn where extensive care was given. On the next day he gave money to the innkeeper to cover the expenses and opened his checkbook for any further cost. Jesus after telling this story then asked the question, "Who do you think proved to be a neighbor to this man?"*

Before answering the obvious, I would like to take these things under consideration.

First, according to the parable we meet our neighbor in the troubled stranger presently before us. The ancient road from Jerusalem down to Jericho was a dangerous road. On the road, robbers lived in the caves along the way and people traveling this road were many times in great danger. This road reaches all the way to St. Louis where there is no safe road. Ours is a time where most anything can happen at any time at any place. One quick viewing of the evening news points to this truth. Crime and violence are no longer isolated in a particular part of town, it's everywhere. The only way that remedy can be found is that people have got to get their heads out of the sand and ask the critical question, "Who is our neighbor?" The answer will be just as plain to them as it was to the lawyer in this story; "The one who shows compassion, the one who is near us, these are our neighbors. The one who is before us that we can not avoid is our neighbor. Regardless of race, creed or color, their need should evoke our response. As Christians we

have a moral obligation to do all that is within our power to ac-
commodate persons who are in need. No one can be neighbor
to everybody, but anyone should be neighbor when called
upon. Our neighbor is the one who is immediately before us.

Secondly, the neighbor can be avoided even in the name of
religion. In the parable the two religious leaders saw the
wounded man and both crossed on the other side on their way
to the temple to honor their religious duties. They fit the de-
scription of those who my pastor says "pass up opportunities
to *be* the church, on the *way* to church." Religious busyness often tramples over human need. When law comes before love,
"ritualism," "institutionalism," and "formalism" will prevail.
However, when love is at the core of one's essence while following Jesus, one can not help but stop and respond to the human hurt. The Christian sees, in the face of those who are hurting, Jesus, and to walk away from them is to walk away from
Jesus.

It is not a requirement to ask people how they got into such
a predicament, just help first. Life is an ever-bending road. All
of us can say where we have been, but none of us can tell
where we will end up. You can start the day on the mountain-
top and one phone call can put you in the valley. It may be that
you do not need the help of a neighbor now, but now is not permanent. Therefore, regardless of our religious affiliations or
cultural make up or social status, when we meet people on
life's journey who have been abused, it is our responsibility as
neighbors to help. Jesus said, "*Inasmuch as you have done
unto the least of them you have done it unto me.*" Matthew
25:45

Thirdly, help often comes from unlikely sources. There are
two surprises in this story in terms of how the wounded man
received help. The first is that we are surprised that the priest
and Levite did not help, but instead crossed over on the other
side. Secondly, we are surprised that the Samaritan did help

and did not leave until the man was properly cared for. The Samaritan, this despised half-breed, had vision that transcended cultural differences to see a person in need. The Samaritan did not report this to a committee and turn the report into weeks of discussion on how to help people in need, he did it himself. He was not willing to hand this man's future to somebody else, he took the responsibility to restore. Perhaps he looked at the man and saw the history of his own mistreatment and responded faithfully by helping. Sometimes one's motivation is a result of their remembering. If we can somehow remember not to forget that we, too, were once in a position unable to help ourselves and God used somebody to help us along the way, we would be quick to help others.

So after telling the story Jesus asked the lawyer, "Who do you think proved to be a neighbor to the man who fell into the hands of robbers?" He responded by saying the one who showed compassion. Jesus said, "Go and do likewise."

No one can do this for everybody, but those who claim to know Jesus as Savior and Lord had better do it for somebody. Amen.

Bibliography

Aden, Leroy & Ellen Harold J. *Turning Points in Pastoral Lane.* Grand Rapids, MI: Baker Book House, 1990.

Ammerman, Nancy Tatom. *Congregations and Community.* New Brunswick, NJ: Rutgers University Press, 1997.

Aquinas Institute of Theology Faculty. *In The Company of Preachers.* Collegeville, MN: The Liturgical Press, 1993.

Barna, George. *User Friendly Church.* Ventura, CA: Regal Books, A Division of Gospel Light, 1991.

Bass, Dorothy C. *Practicing Our Faith.* San Francisco: Jersey-Bass Publishers, 1997.

Bayer, Charles H. *A Guide to Liberation Theology for Middle Class Congregations.* St. Louis: CBP Press, 1986.

Behar, Ruth. *The Vulnerable Observer.* Boston: Beacon Press, 1996

Berry, Hugh B. *Being a Welcoming Congregation.* Louisville: National Ministries Division, Presbyterian Church, 1996.

Best, Thomas & Robra Martin. *Ecclesiology & Ethics.* Geneva: WCC Publications, 1997.

Birch, Bruce C. & Lorri L. Rasmussen. *Bible and Ethics in the Christian Life.* Minneapolis: Augsbury, 1989.

Blount, Brian K. *Go Preach.* Maryknoll, New York: ORBIS Books, 1998.

Bosch, David J. *Transforming Mission.* Maryknoll, New York: ORBIS Books, 1995.

94   *Bibliography*

Bloy, Jr. Myron B. *The Crisis of Cultural Change*. New York: The Seabury Press, 1965.

Bratcher, Dennis. *Travelers and Strangers*. Christian Resource Institute. Copyright, 1998.

Browning, Dan S. *Religious Ethics and Pastoral Care*. Philadelphia: Fortress Press, 1983.

Brueggeman, Walter. *The Land*. Philadelphia: Fortress Press, 1977.

Buttirck, David A. *Captive Voice*. Louisville, KY: Westminster John Knox Press, 1994.

———. *Preaching Jesus Christ*. Philadelphia: Fortress Press, 1998.

Buttry, Daniel. *Peace Ministry: A Handbook For Local Churches*. Valley Forge, PA: Judson Press, 1995.

Campolo, Anthony. *20 Hot Potatoes Christians are Afraid to Touch*. Dallas: Word Publishing, c1988.

Cone, James H. *A Black Theology of Liberation*. Maryknoll, New York: ORBIS Books, 1970.

———. *God of the Oppressed*. Minneapolis: Seabury Press, Inc., 1975.

Corbett, Jack & Elizabeth Smith. *Becoming a Prophetic Community*. Atlanta: John Knox Press, 1971.

Cowles, Ben Thomson. *Free To Be Responsible*. Pasadena: Hope Publishing House, 1990.

Craddock, Fred B. *Overhearing the Gospel*. Nashville: Abingdon Press, 1986.

Dash, Michael, Jonathan Jackson & Stephen Rasor. *Hidden Wholeness*. Cleveland: United Church Press, 1997.

DeYoung, Curtiss Paul. *Coming Together*. Valley Forge, PA: Judson Press, 1995.

Dorman, William and Ronald Allen. *Preaching and Hospitality*. Quarterly Review 14, 1994.

Dykstra, Craig *Growing In the Life of Faith*. Louisville: Geneva Press.

Eger, Richard C. *Pastoral Care Under The Cross*. St. Louis.: CPH, 1994.

Frazier, E. Franklin. *The Negro Church in America*. New York: Schocken Book, 1974.

Furniss, George M. *The Social Context of Pastoral Care.* Louisville: Westminster John Knox Press, 1994.

Geitz, Elizabeth Rankin. Entertaining Angels. Harrisburg, PA: Morehouse Publishing, 1993.

Gerkin , Charles V. *Widening The Horizons.* Philadelphia: Westminster John Knox Press, 1986.

Gros, Jeffery. *The Search for Visible Unity.* The Pilgrim Press. New York, 1984.

Gustafason, James M. *The Church As Moral Decision Maker.* Philadelphia/Boston: PilgrimPress, 1970.

———. *Ethics from a Theocentric Perspective.* Chicago: University of Chicago Press, 1981.

Halverson, Delia. *The Gift of Hospitality.* St. Louis: Chalice Press, 1999.

Halverwas, Stanley & William H Willimon. *Where Resident Aliens Live.* Nashville: Abingdon Press, 1996.

Hessel, Dieter T. *Social Ministry.* Westminster Press, 1992.

Hodgson, Peter C. *Revisioning The Church.* Philadelphia: Fortress Press, 1988.

Hoffman, Gerald J. *How Your Congregation Can Become a More Hospitable Community.* Minneapolis: Augsbury Fortress, 1990.

Hogg, Richard W. *One World One Mission.* New York: Friendship Press, 1960.

Hollander, Edwin P. *Leadership Dynamics.* Philadelphia: The Free Press, 1978.

Holwerda, David E. *Jesus and Israel.* Grand Rapids: William B. Eerdmans Publishing Company, 1995.

Hunter III, George G. *The Contagious Congregation.* Nashville: Abingdon Press, 1979.

Ignatieff, Michael. *The Needs of Strangers.* New York: Viking Penquin, 1985.

James, Linda L. Pickens. *Strangers into Friends.* Nashville: Abingdon Press, 1999.

Jensen, Richard A. *Telling the Story.* Minneapolis: Augsburg Publishing House, 1980.

Jersild, Paul. *Making Moral Decision.* Minneapolis: Fortress Press, 1990.

Keifert, Patrick R. *The Other: Hospitality to the Stranger, Levinas, And Multicultural Mission, A Public Theology of Worship and Evangelism.* Minneapolis: Fortress Press, 1991.
——. *Welcoming the Stranger.* Minneapolis: Fortress Press, 1992.
——. *Ethics And Theology From The Other Side.* Washington D.C.: University Press of America, 1979.
Kelly, George Anthony, 1916. *The Christian Role in Today's Society.* New York: Random House, 1967.
Lane, Thomas G. *The Sense of Preaching.* Atlanta: John Knox Press, 1988.
Lebacqz, Karen. *Justice in an Unjust World.* Minneapolis: Augsburg Publishing House, 1978.
Lincoln, Eric C. & Lawrence Mamiya. *The Black Church in the African American Experience.* Durham: Duke University Press, 1993.
Marty, Martin E. *The One and the Many.* Cambridge, MA: Harvard University Press, 1997.
Massey, James Earl. *The Burdensome Joy of Preaching.* Nashville, TN: Abingdon Press, 1998.
Mathews, Shailer. *Jesus on Social Institutions.* Philadelphia: Fortress Press, 1971.
Mitchell, Henry H. *Black Preaching: The Recovery of a Powerful Art.* Nashville, TN: Abingdon Press, 1990.
Moltman, Jurgen. *The Church In the Power of The Spirit.* San Francisco: Harper, 1975.
Morgan, Peter M. *Story Weaving.* St. Louis, MO: C.B.P. Press, 1986.
Niebuhr, H. Richard. *Christ and Culture.* New York: Schocken Books, 1974.
Niebuhr, Reinhold. *Faith and Politics.* New York: George Braziller, Inc., 1968.
Nouven, Henri J. M. *A Cry for Mercy.* Garden City, NY: Doubleday and Company, Inc., 1983.
——. *Reaching Out: Three Movements of the Spiritual Life.* Garden City, NY: Doubleday & Company, Inc., 1986.
——. *Lifesigns.* Garden City, NY: Doubleday and Company, Inc., 1989.

———. *With Burning Hearts.* New York: ORBIS Books Maryknoll, 1994.

Oglesby, Enoch Hammond. *O Lord Move This Mountain.* St. Louis: Charles Press, 1998.

Ogletree, Thomas W. *Hospitality to the Stranger.* Philadelphia: Fortress Press, 1985.

Oswald, Ray M. and Speed B. Leas. *The Inviting Church.* Herndon, VA: Alban Institute, 1999.

Ottati, Douglas F. *Jesus Christ and Christian Vision.* Louisville, KY: Westminster John Knox Press, 1989.

Palmer, Parker J. *The Company of Strangers.* New York: Crossroad, 1999.

Paris, Peter J. *The Social Teaching of the Black Church.* Philadelphia: Fortress Press, 1985.

Patterson, Stephen J. *The God of Jesus.* Harrisburg, PA: Trinity Press International, 1998.

Powers, Edward A. *Sights of Shalom.* Philadelphia: United Church Press, 1973.

Roberts, J. Deotis. *Roots of A Black Future Family and Church.* Philadelphia: The Westminster Press, 1980.

———. *Black Theology in Dialogue.* Philadelphia: The Westminster Press, 1987.

Rupprecht, David & Ruth. *Radical Hospitality.* Phillipsburg, NJ: Presbyterian and Reformed Publishing Company, 1983.

Sang, C. S. *Jesus and the Reign of God.* Minneapolis: Fortress Press, 1993.

Scaer, David P. *The Sermon on the Mount.* St. Louis: Concordia Publishing House, 1994.

Schaller, Lyle E. *The Seven-Day a Week Church.* Nashville: Abingdon Press, 1992.

Smith, Charles Wallace. *The Church in the Life of the Black Family.* Valley Forge: Judson Press, 1985.

Smith, Kenneth L. and Ira G. Zepp Jr. *Search for the Beloved Community.* Judson Press: Valley Forge, 1974.

Sterba, James P. *Morality in Practice.* Newton, Kansas: Wadsworth Publishing Company, 1991.

Steward, Carlyle Fielding III. *African American Church Growth.* Nashville: Abingdon Press, 1994

Stutzman, Ervin R. *Welcome.* Scottsdale, PA: Herald Press, 1973

Swanson, Rogers K. and Shirley F. Clement. *The Faith Sharing Congregation.* Nashville, TN: Discipleship Resources 1996

Thurman, Howard. *Jesus And the Disinherited.* Richmond, IN: Friends United Press 1976

Walker, Wyatt Tee. *The Soul of Black Worship.* New York: Martin Luther King Fellows Press, 1984

Washington, Preston Robert. *God's Transforming Spirit Black Church Renewal.* Valley Forge: Judson Press, 1988

Welsh, Clement. *Preaching in a New Key.* Philadelphia: Pilgrim Press Book, 1974

Westerhoff, John H. III. *Living the Faith Community.* San Francisco: Harper and Rare Publishers, 1985

Willimon, William H. *With God and Generous Hearts.* Nashville, TN: The Upper Room,

———. *Sunday Dinner.* Nashville, TN: The Upper Room, 1981

Word, Harry F. *The Social Creed of the Churches.* New York. The Abingdon Press, 1914

Notes

1. Anthony Jones (Associate Minister at Shalom Church).
2. Brueggemann, Walter, *The Land.* (Philadelphia: Fortress Press, 1977).
3. Rassmussen, Larry and Birch, Bruce. *Bible and Ethics in the Christian Life* (Minneapolis: Augsbury, 1989).
4. ibid., Rasmussen and Birch, 138.
5. ibid., Rasmussen and Birch, 140.
6. Cone, James, *A Black Theology of Liberation,* (Mary Knoll: Orbis Books, 1970).
7. ibid., Cone.
8. ibid., Cone, 128.
9. ibid., Cone, 128.
10. ibid., Rasmussen/Birch.
11. Oglesby, Enoch. *Ethics and Theology From the Other Side* (Washington, DC: University Press, 1979).
12. ibid.
13. Cone, James. *God of the Oppressed* (Minneapolis: Seabury Press, 1975).
14. ibid., Oglesby, 40.
15. ibid.
16. ibid., Oglesby, 36–43.
17. Gustafson, James M. Ethics *From a Theocentric Perspective* (Chicago: University of Chicago Press, 1981).

18. Ogletree, Thomas W. Hospitality to the Stranger (Philadelphia: Fortress Press, 1985).

19. ibid. Ogletree, 4-5.

20. Nouwen, Henri J.M. *Reaching Out: Three Movements of the Spiritual Life* (Garden City: Doubleday & Company, Inc., 1986).

21. ibid., Nouwen, 103–104.

22. Nouwen, Henri J. *Reaching Out* (Garden City: Image Books, 1986).

23. ibid., Ogletree, 3.

24. Holwerda, David E. *Jesus in Israel, One Covenant or Two?* (Grand Rapids: William B. Eerdmans, 1995).

25. ibid., Holwerda, 125.

26. Nouwen, Henri, *With Burning Hearts* (Maryknoll: Orbis Books, 1994)

27. Palmer, Parker *The Company of Strangers* (New York: Crossword, 1999).

28. Keifert, Patrick, *Welcoming the Stranger* (Minneapolis: Fortress Press, 1992).

29. Frazier, E. Franklin, *The Negro Church in America* (New York: Schoken Books, 1974).

30. Paris, Peter, *The Social Teaching of the Black Church* (Philadephia: Fortress Press, 1985).

31. Smith, Kenneth L. and Tra G. Zepp, Jr. *Search for the Beloved Community* (Valley Forge: Judson Press, 1974).

32. ibid., Smith and Zepp 119.

33. ibid. Smith and Zepp, 131.

34. Lebacqz, Karen, *Justice in an Unjust World* (Minneapolis: Augsburg, 1987).

35. Lebacqz, Karen, ibid., 150.

36. ibid Lebacqz, Karen.

37. Lebacqz, Karen ibid.,. 150.

38. Oglesby, E. Hammond, *O Lord Don't Move This Mountain* (St. Louis: Charles Press, 1988).

39. ibid. Olgesby page 57.

40. Birch, Bruce & Lori Rasmussen, *Bible and Ethics in the Christian Life* (Minneapolis: Augsbury, 1965).

41. Hodgeson, Peter, *Revisioning the Church* (Fortress Press: Philadelphia, 1988).

42. Cone, James, *A Black Theology of Liberation* (Maryknoll: Orbis Books, 1970).

43. Geitz, Elizabeth Rankin, *Entertaining Angels* (Harrisburg: Morehouse Publishing, 1993).

44. Nouwen, Henri, *Reaching Out: Three Movements of Spiritual Life* (Garden City: Doubleday, 1986).

45. William E. Dorman and Ronald Allen, *Preaching and Hospitality.*

46. Halverson, Delia *The Gift of Hospitality* (St. Louis: Chalice Press, 1999).

47. Lane, Thomas *The Sense of Preaching* (Atlanta: John Knox Press, 1988).

48. ibid., Lane.

49. ibid., Palmer.